Safer cities and domestic burglary

by

Paul Ekblom,
Ho Law
and Mike Sutton
with assistance from Paul Crisp
and Richard Wiggins

A Research and Statistics Directorate Report

Home Office
Research and
Statistics
Directorate

London: Home Office

Home Office Research Studies

The Home Office Research Studies are reports on research undertaken by or on behalf of the Home Office. They cover the range of subjects for which the Home Secretary has responsibility. Titles in the series are listed at the back of this report (copies are available from the address on the back cover). Other publications produced by the Research and Statistics Directorate include Research Findings, the Research Bulletin, Statistical Bulletins and Statistical Papers.

The Research and Statistics Directorate

The Directorate consists of three Units which deal with research and statistics on Crime and Criminal Justice, Offenders and Corrections, Immigration and General Matters; the Programme Development Unit; the Economics Unit; and the Operational Research Unit.

 The Research and Statistics Directorate is an integral part of the Home Office, serving the Ministers and the department itself, its services, Parliament and the public through research, development and statistics. Information and knowledge from these sources informs policy development and the management of programmes; their dissemination improves wider public understanding of matters of Home Office concern.

First published 1996

Application for reproduction should be made to the Information and Publications Group, Room 201, Home Office, 50 Queen Anne's Gate,London SW1H 9AT

©Crown copyright 1996 ISBN 1 85893 894 5
ISSN 0072 6435

Foreword

Phase 1 of the £30 million Safer Cities Programme, funded and managed by the Home Office, ran from 1988 to 1995, as the flagship of crime prevention policy. A Treasury requirement was that the impact of the Programme as a whole be evaluated, and Resesrch and Statistics Directorate (RSD), in an early example of a collaborative project between the then Research and Planning Unit and Statistics, took on the job. Aware that evaluations of major initiatives were at risk of delivering unclear answers, or of erroneously contributing to a 'nothing works' view of policy, the evaluation team made strenuous efforts to design a critical but fair test of Safer Cities. Taking this further, they aimed to provide quantitative estimates of cost-effectiveness. Safer Cities schemes against domestic burglary were judged to provide the most readily-evaluated activity because several hundred such schemes were implemented, practice was well-developed and measurement was relatively straightforward.

The evaluation strategy was simple. It involved comparing changes in risk of burglary in large numbers of areas with differing levels of anti-burglary action, against areas (in the Safer Cities themselves and in other, equivalent cities) with no action. Realising the strategy, however, was challenging. It required breaking new ground in linking 'micro' analysis of small areas, and the Safer Cities action they received, to the 'macro' scale of cities and to the overall performance of a major programme of prevention. An exceptionally wide range of data sources were drawn on, including crime surveys and recorded crime statistics (the outcome measures), the 1991 Census, a comprehensive Management Information System which the evaluation team helped to design, and maps of local anti-burglary action. The data-collection operation was on an 'industrial' scale. (The effort involved in assembling the local recorded crime information in particular revealed just how far the police have to go in providing the infrastructure to support routine local or national evaluations of anti-crime measures of whatever sort.) A Geographic Information System was used to draw all this data together, and state-of-the-art statistical modelling was employed to produce quantified estimates of impact whilst taking account of background trends in crime and incidental differences between areas. Given the complexity of the analysis, the evaluation team devoted considerable effort to finding ways of presenting the results graphically.

The two very different outcome measures produced conclusions which were remarkably similar. Under most conditions, but particularly in areas of high crime risk typical of cities, the cost of preventing a burglary through Safer Cities action was less than the financial cost of that burglary to victims and the state. Impact on people's worry about burglary was less clear-cut, depending on both the amount of action in their neighbourhood and whether they were aware of any such activity. Nevertheless, in a context where in the past few large-scale interventions against social problems seem to have had much measurable effect, the overall picture is one of good news.

Results and wider experience from this evaluation were fed into planning the implementation and evaluation of Phase 2 of the Safer Cities Programme, now the responsibility of DOE through the Single Regeneration Budget. The methods pioneered are now available for assessment of other large-scale initiatives – a task which should become easier as the police pursue systematic development of 'geo-referenced' and computerised crime data.

The results of the evaluation are fully reported in the summary to this report (also published separately as Research Finding 42). The main purpose of the report is to provide a technical account of the data collected, the methods developed and the analysis conducted.

CHRISTOPHER NUTTALL
DIRECTOR, RESEARCH AND STATISTICS
December 1996

Acknowledgements

This evaluation, given its use of many data sources and development of new methods, relied on an unprecedented range of people.

In the Home Office, Tom Ellis and Justin Russell provided ideas and research support in the earlier stages of the evaluation. Judith Cotton, Nicola Dowds, Tim Edwards, Colin Gordon and Roy Reece at various stages collected and entered data. Collaboration from a number of police forces and local authorities also made this possible. David Godfrey and David Mann gave significant help on our computer installation. Tim Hope, Trevor Benn and Kathleen Shaw contributed strategic ideas. Simon Field and Catriona Mirrlees-Black respectively provided cost and British Crime Survey data. Roy Walmsley, Pat Mayhew and Bob Butcher provided immediate management support, often at difficult times. Pat Mayhew in particular contributed a great deal in sharpening the analysis and rendering the drafting of complex material more intelligible. Prof. Nick Tilley (attached to Police Research Group) contributed useful ideas and helpful comments at various stages. Other colleagues in PRG collaborated on the design of the Management Information System and the transfer of its data. Colleagues in the Crime Prevention Agency (formerly Unit) channelled vital information on Safer Cities action from the projects and aided quality control. They proved helpful and understanding in reconciling the constraints of research with the demands of policy. The Safer Cities project teams willingly supplied information and useful opinions.

Consultants or other organisations to whom we turned for advice or employed for specific tasks included:

- The South-East Regional Research Laboratory, London University (John Shepherd and Prof. David Rhind), for advice on Geographic Information Systems

- OPCS (Bob Butcher and David Elliot), regarding sample size and statistical power; also provision of 1991 Census data

- Department of the Environment for Index of Local Conditions data

- School of Advanced Urban Studies, Bristol University (Prof. Murray Stewart), on the evaluation strategy and implementation process

- North-Western Regional Research Laboratory, Lancaster University (David Howes and colleagues), for development of the action scoring software – a particularly challenging and pathfinding task crucial to bringing all sources of action data together in the right form

- ESRI UK Ltd (Melissa Phillips) for supplying the ArcInfo Geographic Information System, training and start-up consultancy

- MORI Ltd (Kai Rudat and Mark Speed), for the main surveys

- RSGB Ltd (Philip Mercieca) for pilot surveys

- GDC Ltd (Graham Hunt) for digitisation of beat boundary data, plus supply of digitised Enumeration District boundaries

- Centre for Applied Statistics, Lancaster University (Prof. Richard Davies and Granville Tunnicliffe-Wilson), for advice on statistical modelling and presentation of results

- The Institute of Education Multilevel Models Project, University of London (Prof. Harvey Goldstein, Jon Rasbach and Min Yang), for supplying ML3E (our analytical software), advice on design, initial training and subsequent (heavily-drawn on) support

- Prof. Ken Pease (University of Huddersfield) for much advice on design, statistics, analysis and interpretation, and also for acting as independent assessor for this report.

Our two major collaborators deserve special mention. Paul Crisp (now at Ordnance Survey) helped integrate the database, and install and get working the action scoring system – a pivotal task. Richard Wiggins (Reader, Social Statistics Research Unit, City University) contributed significantly to the design, training and conduct of the multi-level modelling analysis.

PAUL EKBLOM
HO LAW
MIKE SUTTON

Contents

Summary

Phase 1 of the Safer Cities Programme set up just over 500 schemes to prevent domestic burglary. Most upgraded physical security, though some mounted community-oriented initiatives as well. The schemes usually centred on local neighbourhoods or estates. The results of a major evaluation of nearly 300 of the schemes are reported here.

Key points

- Overall, the schemes reduced burglary and were cost-effective. Simply implementing action in a police beat reduced local risks by nearly 10 per cent.

- Physical security measures against burglary seemed to work independently. But community-oriented activities (e.g., to increase awareness and promote crime prevention) needed reinforcement with action against other types of crime, or against crime in general. Taken as a whole, the burglary schemes worked better in this wider context.

- The overall cost of each burglary prevented was about £300 in very high-crime areas. It was about £900 when risks were at the lower end of the scale. The average financial cost of a burglary to the state and the victim was about £1,100. Grossed up, a very approximate estimate for the total benefit from Safer Cities burglary action was 56,000 burglaries prevented at a saving of about £31 million – not far short of the cost of the entire Programme.

- Reduction in burglary risk was greater where there was more intense burglary action but to achieve these bigger falls cost disproportionately more. 'Marginal cost' estimates per extra prevented burglary ranged from about £1,100 in the highest risk areas to about £3,300 in the lower-risk ones. In monetary terms extra expenditure was justified only in high risk areas but there are other considerations (see below).

- Low-intensity action seemed to displace some burglaries to nearby areas, and to cause burglars to switch to other property crime within the actual scheme area. But when action was of moderate intensity or more, neither problem occurred. In fact, adjacent areas also benefitted from some reduction in burglary, and other crime decreased in scheme areas.

- Although only a few people were aware of preventive action in their area, if they were aware, and the action was intensive, they worried less about burglary. If they were aware but it was low level action, they were actually more worried than before.

- People's perceptions of their area's quality improved only where action was most intensive.

The Safer Cities Programme

Phase 1 of Safer Cities started in 1988 and ended in Autumn 1995. It aimed to reduce crime and fear of crime, and to create safer environments for economic and community life to flourish. Safer Cities was part of the Government's wider plan, Action for Cities, set up to deal with the multiple problems of some larger urban areas.

Safer Cities was locally based and took a 'partnership' or multi-agency approach. In each of 20 cities or boroughs, the Home Office funded a project co-ordinator and a small team recruited locally from various professional backgrounds. Each team was guided by steering committees representing local government, the police, probation, voluntary bodies and commerce.

The projects tackled a range of crime problems – e.g., domestic and commercial burglary, domestic violence, vehicle crime, shop theft, disorder, and sometimes fear of crime. Some projects focused on the city as a whole (e.g., publicity campaigns and multi-agency co-ordination of strategies). But most schemes were local and focused on vulnerable people, particular institutions or localities.

A variety of local organisations were invited to bid for funds from Safer Cities grants (up to £250,000 annually per city). Some 3,600 schemes were started, using £30 million, of Safer Cities money in direct and administrative costs. Just over 500 schemes focused on domestic burglary – spending £4.4 million in Safer Cities grants.

A problem solving approach

All Safer Cities action was meant to take a rational, problem-solving approach:

- analysing crime and other data to identify local crime patterns and set objectives

- adopting tailor-made preventive measures, drawing on a range of methods

- evaluating what was done and making changes as necessary.

Safer Cities action against burglary

This evaluation centred on domestic burglary – an aspect of Safer Cities where the impact on crime could be more readily measured. Domestic burglary was often targeted by co-ordinators, preventive practice is relatively well-developed, and burglary schemes tend to have localised effects. Just under 300 of the total 500 burglary schemes were underway or completed by Summer 1992. This evaluation focuses on these schemes which consisted of:

- target-hardening (e.g., door, window and fencing improvements; entry systems; alarms; and security lighting) – used in three in four schemes

- community-oriented action (e.g., supplying 'tool libraries' to help DIY security installation, fostering Neighbourhood Watch and property marking, employing workers to raise burglary awareness among householders and local agencies) – used in nearly one in ten schemes

- other activities e.g., the distribution of leaflets and small house-to-house surveys.

The amount spent per scheme ranged from a few pounds for leaflets to over £100,000 for major target-hardening. The number of households covered ranged from a single block to a whole district. The average number of households covered was 5,200. About one in three schemes had 'levered-in' funds from other sources as well as Safer Cities money (although this was not consistently recorded). More Safer Cities money itself was spent in the schemes with levered-in funds – so Safer Cities funds were not simply being used to substitute for other sources.

How much money was spent in 300 schemes

All 300 schemes (average)
Safer Cities money per scheme £8,700
No. of households covered   5,200

Two-thirds schemes with no levered funds
Safer Cities money   £7,300

One-third schemes with levered-in funds
Safer Cities money   £11,300
Levered-in funds   £17,800

The evaluation approach

Some individual Safer Cities burglary schemes have been evaluated (Tilley and Webb, 1994). But an assessment of the cost-effectiveness of the schemes as a whole provides the best picture of what a large-scale prevention programme can do. Outcome was measured in two ways:

- before-and-after surveys – 7,500 household interviews were carried out in over 400 high-crime neighbourhoods in 11 Safer Cities and eight comparison cities. The 'before' surveys took place in late-1990, the 'after' ones in late-1992. Although it was not known at the start of the evaluation where action would be initiated, in the event, the surveyed areas covered a sufficient number of schemes – 96 of the 300 set up

- local police crime statistics covering the period 1987 – 1992. They encompassed 700 police beats in 14 Safer Cities, and included coverage of 240 burglary schemes. There were also city-level statistics in nine comparison cities.

The two sources were complementary. The police figures covered a wider area, and a longer period. The surveys provided information about householders' experience of crime whether or not reported to the police, and their perceptions about crime.

The average effects of burglary action in small areas were studied by looking for changes in risk in:

- Safer Cities areas where nothing was done

- Safer Cities areas with burglary schemes of varying 'intensity' (see box below)

- a set of comparison cities.

Scheme intensity

A universal measure of action input was needed to estimate the effects of a variety of burglary schemes spending different amounts in different ways and covering areas of different sizes. When action took place in an area its 'intensity' was measured by dividing the total amount spent by the total number of households in the area. It was not possible to say which individual households had been the focus of action. Adjustments were also made for how long action had been in place. If more than one scheme covered an area their intensities were combined. Population data from the 1991 Census and scheme data from the Safer Cities Management Information System were also used. Linking all this data needed purpose-built computer software in a Geographic Information System.

Intensive schemes were either costly ones, or more modest ones concentrated on a small area. Including levered funds, the intensity of action in the surveyed areas ranged from 1p to £113 per household. The mean was £16 – relatively few areas exceeded this by much. The range in the police beats was similar, but because the areas were larger, and therefore not always fully covered by schemes, the average was lower, at £4.

The survey results

There was good evidence from the surveys that Safer Cities schemes reduced the risk of burglary in the areas they covered. Table S.1 shows how risks changed across the different types of area. The risks here are the proportion of households burgled once or more in the past year – a 'prevalence' measure.

Table S.1
Changes in burglary risk according to the household surveys

	Safer Cities					Comparison Cities
	No action	*Low intensity*	*Medium intensity*	*High intensity*	*All action areas*	
Percentage of households burgled once or more in last year						
Before	8.9	10.3	12.7	13.4	11.6	12.0
After	10.2	9.3	9.9	7.6	9.1	12.4
Percentage change (Before to After)						
	+15	-10	-22	-43	-21	+3

Between 1990 and 1992, burglary risks in the comparison cities rose by three per cent, In Safer Cities areas where there was no burglary action, risks showed a bigger increase, of 15 per cent. But where there was action, risks fell: by 10 per cent in low-action areas (under £1 of Safer Cities funds per household), 22 per cent in medium-action areas (£1 – £13), and by 43 per cent in high-action areas (over £13). The overall fall was 21 per cent.

The actual changes in burglary in different types of area are shown in Table S.1 but statistical modelling is a more accurate way of assessing the effect of Safer Cities. This takes other factors into account which may coincidentally influence crime levels, and thus bias the result. An advanced statistical technique – multi-level modelling – analysed the effect of background trends in crime and demographic differences across areas and between survey respondents. Figure S.1 compares the level of risk in the action areas observed in the 'after' surveys with the risk that would have been expected had the Safer Cities action not been set up but area characteristics and background trends in crime stayed the same. All areas with action (including levered funds for completeness) had a large drop in risk compared to expectations. Risks were 24 per cent less than expected in the 'after' survey in low-action areas, 33 per cent in medium-action areas and 37 per cent in high-action areas.

Figure S.1
Expected and observed risks of burglary from the survey figures

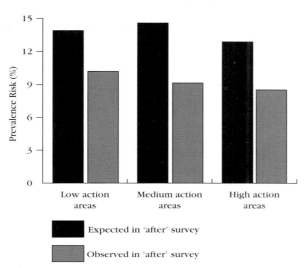

The results from police figures

Police figures gave the same picture as the surveys. Thus, again taking account of area differences and background trends (in particular a widespread drop in crime in about 1987–90 which then reversed), a Safer Cities 'effect' was once more observed. Risks continued broadly as expected until 1990, the year in which action began. Then, in 1991, all police beats in action areas had a reduction in risk. In 1992, risks in high action areas continued to decline. Risks in medium action areas increased a little, but were still below expected. In low action areas risks rose slightly above what was expected, suggesting that where action is insufficiently intensive its effect is short-lived.

The overall picture

Both the survey and police figures showed that the schemes' impact had two distinct components:

- setting up any action substantially reduced burglary risks in the area. Risks fell by nearly 10 per cent in police beats, and by more in the surveyed neighbourhoods, although that estimate can be calculated in different ways, with different results. (Smaller territories of measurement and different samples of schemes could explain the higher estimate in the surveys, although in any case margins of error were large.)

- the more intense the burglary action, the greater the additional drop in risk. This extra marginal reduction was estimated to be 0.5%–1.0% for each extra £1 of action per household in the action area.

Cost-effectiveness

The value of Safer Cities can be assessed by comparing burglary costs with the cost of prevention. The average burglary costs the state and the victim in financial loss (measured in urban areas) about £1,100. This is based on all burglaries, including those not recorded by the police and does not allow for any psychological cost. Burglary prevention costs were estimated from the statistical models but, as with any cost-effectiveness calculations, assumptions had to be made. A critical one was how long a 'Safer Cities effect' would last – estimated at two years.

The estimates from the recorded crime figures are on the lower curve in Figure S.2. (The survey ones are very similar.) The level of risk for which costs of prevented burglaries are shown are the annual number of burglary incidents per 100 households. This is an incidence risk rather than the prevalence one earlier, to take account of the fact that some households are burgled more than once in a year. The fact that more burglaries happen than are recorded by the police is also allowed for in the costing.

Figure S.2
Cost effectiveness estimates: results from police figures

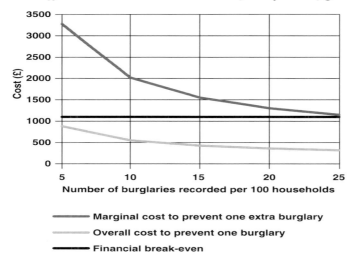

Marginal cost to prevent one extra burglary
Overall cost to prevent one burglary
Financial break-even

As might be expected, it was cheaper to prevent a burglary in areas with higher burglary risk. Thus, the amount spent from both Safer Cities and other funds was about £300 per prevented burglary at the highest end of the risk scale (25 burglaries per 100 homes in a year). It was about £900 at the lower end (five burglaries – roughly equivalent to the national average). Grossing up to an estimated total spend on local domestic burglary schemes of £6.6 million (including levered funds) produces a very rough estimate of 56,000 burglaries prevented by the Safer Cities Programme, and a resultant saving to victims and state of £31 million. This is of the same order as the entire cost of the Programme.

The overall cost figures show that, at levels of risk typical of cities, preventive action is worth implementing. Once it is agreed to take action in an area, consideration must be given to whether it is worth spending more to try and achieve a greater reduction in burglaries. This will involve estimating what are known as 'marginal' costs. One would expect marginal costs to be higher than overall costs because they discount what is achieved simply by a scheme being in place. This proved to be the case.

The marginal cost of preventing a burglary additional to those prevented by the schemes, as they typically operated, can be estimated with the statistical models. This marginal cost (the upper curve on Figure S.2) would range from about £3,300 in lower-risk conditions to £1,100 in higher-risk ones. The preventive cost in higher-risk areas, then, matches what a burglary costs state and victim financially. The implication is that more intense schemes only offer good value for money in higher-risk areas. But taking into account psychological costs would broaden the range where value was achieved.

Displacement

Reducing burglaries in a scheme area sometimes led to burglaries being displaced to adjacent areas. Where this occurred, the overall positive effect of Safer Cities was diminished, as well as its cost-effectiveness. However, this displacement did not always happen. Rather, where burglary action was of moderate or higher intensity (estimated at over £4 per household), the preventive effect reached beyond the area covered by the scheme – so-called 'diffusion of benefit'. But even with the sophisticated methods employed, it was not possible to estimate how the savings in the target areas and some of the adjacent areas balanced against the losses from displacement in others.

Displacement to different forms of offending – 'crime switch' – was also assessed. The results indicated that when burglary action was low intensity, some switch to other property offences did occur. But when action was of moderate or higher intensity (over £5 per household), there seemed to be a reduction in the risk of other property crimes too.

An extra benefit of burglary action in an area was the protection it appeared to afford against 'inward' displacement from neighbouring burglary schemes. It also protected against 'crime switch' to burglary when Safer Cities action had been taken against other crime types.

Worry about burglary

The before and after surveys asked householders how worried they were about burglary. They were also asked if they were aware of any crime prevention initiatives in their area. After the Safer Cities action, people generally showed no increase in awareness that action against crime had been taken in their area but those interviewed would not necessarily be in a household which had been targetted. Also, awareness of action is generally low with any preventive initiative. The exception was in high-intensity areas, which showed a marked increase in awareness.

Those individuals who were aware of action worried less about burglary where the action was intensive. However, where action was of a low level, those who were aware of action were actually more worried than before. This may be because they were alerted to a burglary problem, but did not see it being tackled effectively. A similar finding was that people's views about the quality of their area only improved where action was greatest.

The value of a comprehensive approach

Two or more Safer Cities schemes were often combined in a locality. Of the burglary action areas covered by the surveys, a third had target-hardening schemes alone; a third had other (usually community-oriented) burglary action alone, and a third had combined action. Most of the burglary action areas also had Safer Cities action targetted on other crimes or crime in general (a factor incorporated in the costs). Disentangling the combinations which worked best against burglary was difficult. The survey data provided some indications.

Target-hardening reduced burglary under all conditions. Purely community-oriented burglary action only worked in tandem with action against other crimes. The best combination was when all elements were present. When burglary action was considered as a whole, the support of action against other crimes seemed more generally important. Like other studies, then, this evaluation suggests a comprehensive approach is best, although target-hardening could work alone.

The lessons for policy and practice

This evaluation bears on several key questions about burglary prevention programmes such as those in Safer Cities. The findings are relevant to both central policy and local practice, particularly in regard to action through co-ordinated local initiatives in a partnership context.

Is co-ordinated local action against domestic burglary worthwhile?

Action of the type taken in Safer Cities (Phase 1) was cost-effective in the areas, with the higher burglary risks typical of cities, where burglary schemes were targetted. As mentioned earlier, there was some evidence that this cost-effectiveness was reduced in places because burglars shifted their attention elsewhere. But there were also signs, at least when action was intensive, that burglars avoided a wider area than that in which the action occurred. This increased cost-effectiveness. Whether these losses and gains cancel each other out cannot be assessed with any precision.

A further caveat is that no evidence is available of the cost-effectiveness of other ways of arranging local preventive action, or of wider alternatives such as police patrolling. Careful evaluations of these alternatives are needed.

How did the action work?

The fact that the mere presence of burglary action seems to reduce burglary risk, suggests that 'area' processes are operating rather than those which act to defend individual homes. Offenders, alert to any action in an area, find it unattractive to operate there. Supporting evidence for this comes from two sources:

- the existence of crime displacement to adjacent areas

- the 'protective' influence of existing burglary action in an area against inward displacement from adjacent action, and against 'crime switch' to burglary.

Diffusion of benefit (in areas with more intense action) suggests that offenders are being guided by illusory risks of being caught beyond the boundaries of schemes. But in general, the kind of impact measured may be shorter- rather than longer-term.

Where is it best to target action?

By and large, targetting areas with moderate to high rates of burglary, typical of cities, promises the best returns. The main difficulty in achieving such targetting in future programmes is the lack of readily accessible local crime data. (Obtaining the data, both to supply co-ordinators with local 'crime profiles' of their cities and to support this evaluation, was extremely slow and labour intensive.) Geographic Information Systems would help and, if operated to a common standard, would facilitate local and national evaluations of crime prevention initiatives.

What amount of action is needed?

Generally, the more the better, but it is not entirely straightforward. More intensive schemes seem to:

*   stop displacement of burglaries to other areas

*   have a beneficial spillover effect to other areas

*   prevent switching to other forms of property offending.

They may also give economies of scale in implementation and have a more durable effect.

However, less intense action also had an impact. So in future programmes reducing scheme intensity (by cutting the spend per scheme, or increasing the area each scheme covered) would allow a greater coverage of areas and/or households. But here the impact would be narrower. There seems to be an important threshold of action beneath which, even if burglary is reduced, people's views of their area do not improve, they remain unaware of what is being done, and they continue to worry about burglary. The best estimate of this threshold is a spend of roughly £20 per household in an area. At this intensity, displacement should also be much less of a problem, since it appeared to be countered at about the £4 level upwards.

What sort of action to take?

A comprehensive strategy which combines action against burglary with action against crime in general is most appropriate. It would appear that 'community-oriented' action against burglary should not be introduced alone. In addition, it seems more effective to bring schemes together across adjacent areas. This decreases the chance of burglary being deflected elsewhere, since it is known that burglars tend to be unwilling to travel greater distances.

Well-publicised action is likely to be more effective. This should reassure householders, and send a stronger deterrent message to offenders. But action of the appropriate kind and intensity obviously needs to be taken, not just announced. Finally, publicity should also be handled carefully, to avoid raising unrealistic expectations and causing possible resentment that some households are losing out to others.

1 Introduction

Phase 1 of the Safer Cities Programme was inaugurated in 1988 and wound up in Autumn 1995. Altogether, it cost about £30 million, including £8 million administrative costs. Substantial levered-in funds were also obtained from other sources. Safer Cities was set up as part of Action for Cities, the Government's wider programme to deal with the multiple social, physical and economic problems of some of our larger urban areas. The objectives of Safer Cities were to reduce crime, lessen fear of crime, and create safer cities within which economic enterprise and community life could flourish.

Safer Cities initiatives were locally-based, reflecting an understanding developed since the 1980s that crime is best tackled at the local level (Home Office, 1990b, 1991, 1993b). The initiative also adopted a 'partnership' or multi-agency approach to crime prevention (Home Office, 1990a, 1993a). The Programme was developed in the light of experience of an earlier programme, the 'Five Towns' initiative (Liddle and Bottoms, 1992).

In each of 20 areas – covering cities or boroughs – a local project was set up with a co-ordinator and a small team, whose salaries and overheads were met by the Home Office. Co-ordinators were recruited locally and drawn from a range of backgrounds, including police, social work, probation and local government. The work of each was guided by a steering committee representing local government, police, probation, voluntary bodies and commerce. The committees set the priorities for the project and oversaw implementation (for a discussion of the roles of the co-ordinators and their committees, see Tilley, 1992; Sutton, 1996).

Safer Cities projects featured a wide range of activities, including awareness-raising among citizens and local agencies, and the development of community safety strategies in local government. But at the core of the projects was the initiation of local preventive schemes. These schemes were implemented on the ground by a variety of local organisations, which were invited to bid for funds.[1] The schemes drew on grants from Safer Cities – up to £250,000 annually per city – and other local or national resources. Altogether, Safer Cities initiated some 3,600 schemes at a cost of £22 million.

---

1   Depending on the size of the grant sought, approval could be given by the steering committee itself or referred up
     successively to the Home Office and Treasury.

The preventive action was intended to take the rational, problem-oriented approach developed within crime prevention over the last decade (Tilley, 1993b; Laycock and Tilley, 1995; Sutton, 1996). This 'preventive process' involves several steps:

- analysing crime data and related information to identify local patterns of crime

- setting objectives

- adopting appropriate preventive measures (tailor-made rather than off-the-shelf)

- implementing action

- evaluating what has been done and making changes where necessary.

To take forward this problem-oriented approach, co-ordinators were given a limited amount of training and support from professionals in the Home Office and elsewhere (few co-ordinators had much background in criminology or use of analytic or computing techniques). They were also provided by the Research and Statistics Department with an initial 'crime and social profile' of their area, including a beat-by-beat picture of recorded crime rates. These profiles were time-consuming to produce, which is itself indicative of the poor state of local information generally available. But they aimed to help co-ordinators and their steering committees to develop priorities and set up an action plan regarding which areas and which crimes to target for action.

The schemes deliberately addressed a wide range of crime problems using an equally wide range of methods. The crime problems varied from domestic burglary (the subject of this report) to commercial burglary, assault, domestic violence, vehicle-related theft and shop theft. In some cases the focus was more on fear of crime. Preventive methods included both 'situational' action and offender-oriented action. The former comprised measures such as better security hardware, alarms, improved lighting and surveillance measures. The latter covered youth work, holiday play schemes, credit unions, adventure playgrounds, employment advice, even morality plays in schools. Some schemes focused on the city as a whole (e.g., through publicity campaigns, information initiatives such as crime prevention buses, or multi-agency programmes). Many schemes focused on vulnerable individuals, groups of homes, particular institutions (such as schools and clubs), or particular localities (e.g. housing estates, car parks or city centres).

Coming in the wake of the Government's Financial Management Initiative, the Safer Cities Programme was meant to offer value for money and to be subject to rigorous evaluation.

This report is aimed at a technical audience. Its functions are twofold:

- to substantiate the findings, virtually all of which are presented in the preceding summary (and separately as Research Findings 42 ([Paul Ekblom, Ho Law and Mike Sutton 1996])

- to give more detail of the new methods developed, which may be of use in other evaluations.

The evaluation strategy

Evaluation of Safer Cities has been conducted at a number of levels, for different purposes and therefore to different standards. Co-ordinators themselves were responsible for ensuring that at least a minimal assessment was made of each scheme funded (this was part of the conditions of grant, and an evaluation guide was produced [Youell, 1993]). What is now the Police Research Group in the Home Office evaluated a number of 'themes' such as Safer Cities schemes using CCTV in car parks (Tilley, 1993a) and domestic burglary. This exercise (Tilley and Webb, 1994) aimed at assembling good practice information, used detailed retrospective case studies of ten selected burglary schemes, and in some respects was complementary to the present, much larger-scale evaluation. They also conducted an assessment of the success which projects had in fostering local community safety strategies (Tilley, 1992). This was to facilitate the continuation of local co-ordinated crime prevention after the Safer Cities projects closed as planned.

The focus in the Research and Statistics Department study was on the impact of the Safer Cities Programme as a whole. Our approach was to look at the *typical* scheme – since this provides the best picture of what a large-scale prevention programme is capable of implementing given an essentially untrained set of co-ordinators with varying levels of experience and competence, funding activity implemented on the ground by agencies or groups with equally varied experience. The alternative approach – to pick in advance a set of 'good prospects', or to comb retrospectively for 'success stories' – might say something about good practice, but not much about the cost-effectiveness of the Programme. Tilley and Webb (1994) describe the difficulties in obtaining adequate retrospective data for scheme-level evaluations of anti-burglary action in the Safer Cities context. The Dutch government's attempt to evaluate a set of individual preventive schemes identified in advance met with severe attrition problems as poor implementation, poor data and weak scheme evaluations eliminated many (Polder, 1992; Junger-Tas, 1993). Wider discussions of the difficulties of evaluating crime prevention initiatives are to be found in Ekblom (1990) and Ekblom and Pease (1995).

The evaluation of Safer Cities required us to link measures of *Safer Cities action* to measures of *outcome* – crime and fear. The nature of Safer Cities made this challenging. In particular, many schemes were small in resource terms, or spread thinly over large areas. This meant that the impact of individual schemes was often likely to be modest, and that it was best to consider a large number simultaneously. Changes in crime were also likely to be influenced by local factors, and by background trends at city and national level. These needed to be taken into account as much as possible, otherwise they could mask – or mimic – any impact of Safer Cities. To minimise the risks of delivering inconclusive findings, and to conduct a 'fair test' which balanced the risk of mistakenly reporting success of Safer Cities against that of mistakenly reporting failure, the strategy devised was ground-breaking in several ways (Ekblom, 1992; Ekblom and Pease, 1995). It required the use of state-of-the art computing centring around a Geographic Information System (Ekblom, Howes and Law, 1994) and equally new statistical techniques to look simultaneously at changes in burglary risk over time in households, localities and cities (Ekblom, Sutton and Wiggins, 1993). In the event, we developed a method that was simple in principle, complex and labour-intensive to realise in practice, but (as will be seen) capable of producing straightforward answers.

Domestic burglary was chosen for this report because co-ordinators often targetted it, preventive practice is relatively well-developed, and burglary schemes tend to be local and have localised effects. If the Safer Cities Programme was going to have a measurable impact on crime, we reasoned, it would be on burglary.

Safer Cities action against burglary

Figure 1.1 shows that, by 1995, of the 2,300 Safer Cities schemes in all 20 cities with an identifiable physical target, just over half were targetted on dwellings. Figure 1.2 shows that a third of the schemes which had an identifiable target crime, were targetted on burglary, whether domestic or otherwise.

Figure 1.1 Safer Cities: Physical targets

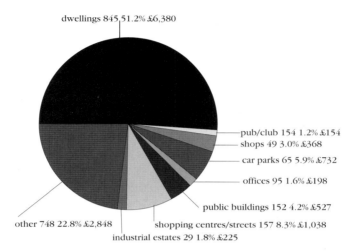

dwellings 845 51.2% £6,380

pub/club 154 1.2% £154
shops 49 3.0% £368
car parks 65 5.9% £732
offices 95 1.6% £198
public buildings 152 4.2% £527
shopping centres/streets 157 8.3% £1,038
industrial estates 29 1.8% £225
other 748 22.8% £2,848

Numbers relate to all 20 Phase 1 Safer Cities as at early 1995. They are i) total number of schemes in a given category; ii) percentage of specified funds spent on that category; iii) total specified funds in £ thousands spent on that category. All numbers refer to specified schemes only: 54% of all schemes were specified on this feature in the Management Information System; 43% of total funds spent on all schemes were so specified.

Figure 1.2 Safer Cities: Target crime types

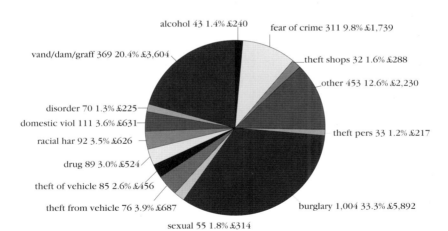

alcohol 43 1.4% £240
fear of crime 311 9.8% £1,739
vand/dam/graff 369 20.4% £3,604
theft shops 32 1.6% £288
other 453 12.6% £2,230
disorder 70 1.3% £225
domestic viol 111 3.6% £631
racial har 92 3.5% £626
theft pers 33 1.2% £217
drug 89 3.0% £524
theft of vehicle 85 2.6% £456
theft from vehicle 76 3.9% £687
burglary 1,004 33.3% £5,892
sexual 55 1.8% £314

Numbers relate to all 20 Phase I Safer Cities as at early 1995. They are i) total number of schemes in a given category; ii) percentage of specified funds spent on that category; iii) total specified funds in £ thousands spent on that category. All numbers refer to specfied schemes only: 88% of all schemes were specified on this feature in the Management Information System; 77% of total funds spent on all schemes were so specified.

Altogether, some 500 schemes were targetted on domestic burglary, spending some £4.4 million of Safer Cities funds and further levered-in funds or in-kind assistance from other local or national sources. Our evaluation, for reasons of timing, focussed on the first 16 cities to be implemented, and on the nearly 300 schemes targetted on domestic burglary at the local level, that were current or completed by Summer 1992. (A further 62 schemes, such as publicity campaigns, were targetted at city level, but these are not considered here as their 'thin spread' is unlikely to have had much impact that was measurable locally.) Of the local schemes, three-quarters focussed on domestic target-hardening (including door, window and fencing improvements, entry systems, and security lighting around individual houses or blocks; normally, a number of weaknesses were tackled together in a security package for the dwellings). Eight per cent were focussed on community-oriented action (e.g., providing crime prevention outreach workers, raising awareness of prevention, fostering neighbourhood watch and property-marking). Offender-oriented action specifically targetted at burglary was rare. The amount spent per scheme varied from a few pounds to over £100,000. The areas which schemes covered ranged from single blocks of flats to whole districts; on average about 5,200 households were covered – equivalent to 26 Enumeration Districts (EDs) from the 1991 Census.

Across burglary schemes as a whole, the average amount of *Safer Cities* funding spent was *£8,700*. But this amount differed according to whether there were additional *levered-in funds* raised from local agencies and institutions, and from other national programmes. Two-thirds of the burglary schemes had no leverage recorded on the Management Information System, and the average Safer Cities funds spent was *£7,300*. For the remaining third of schemes with levered-in funds, the average Safer Cities spend was *£11,300* and the average *levered* supplement *£17,800*. The fact that more Safer Cities money was spent on schemes with levered-in funds indicates that Safer Cities funds were not used to substitute for funds from other sources. (If this had been the case, the Safer Cities funds spent would have been more when levered funds were unavailable.) Interestingly, the levered schemes were on average geographically smaller than the rest (by 53%, or 19 enumeration districts versus 29).

Measuring Safer Cities action

There would be little prospect of finding impact by simply comparing cities. And indeed, examining recorded crime trends in the first 16 Safer Cities and in a matched set of other cities shows – if anything – that the Safer Cities fared somewhat worse in terms of growth in burglary. Rather, a fairer test meant looking for impact where one might expect to find it – at the 'small area' level, in the vicinity of local schemes – and taking account of the *amount* of local action.

Action intensity

To estimate the effects of a variety of burglary schemes spending different amounts in different ways and covering areas of different sizes, we needed a universal measure of action input. Output measures of action, such as numbers of homes secured, numbers of locks fitted etc – were too diverse and too unreliable (see Ekblom and Pease, 1995:649).

Using data from the Safer Cities Management Information System (on the crime targets of each scheme, their start date, and their cost from Safer Cities and levered-in funds), 1991 ED maps of scheme locations supplied by the co-ordinators, and population data from the 1991 Census, an *action intensity score* was calculated for each small area covered in the evaluation. This score represented *the average amount of funds acting on each household over a given year*. For each scheme affecting the area, it took into account the total amount spent, the area over which the scheme was spread, and the length of time each scheme had been operating.[end note 1] The most intensive schemes were either costly ones, or more modest ones concentrated on a small area. If more than one scheme covered an area we added the intensities.

The amount spent was averaged over *all households* in the area because it was not possible to identify which individual household had or had not received action. Besides, measuring Safer Cities impact on areas was felt to be more appropriate.

Besides this 'hard' data on Safer Cities action, 'softer' information of various kinds was used to help guide and interpret analysis. Brief descriptions of each scheme were available on the Management Information System; and open-ended interviews with co-ordinators threw light on the process by which they assigned action to particular locations. In addition, we had a deep knowledge of the Programme over its lifetime. As well as evaluating it, we contributed to the process of targeting action, for example by preparing crime and social profiles. Consequently, contacts with co-ordinators were regular.

Measuring outcome

To measure outcome, two sources of local data were collected: information from sample surveys of adults, and police recorded crime figures. The two sources were complementary, with different strengths and weaknesses

(Appendix 4). The *survey* data is able to focus on smaller areas than the recorded crime data available at realistic cost and effort to this evaluation (Census enumeration districts – EDs, of about 200 households, rather than police beats, of an average 1,700 households). It is richer, covering not just crime victimisation but a wider range of questions on fear, perceptions of crime and security-related behaviour. It links to individual residents' social characteristics, and avoids the reporting and recording shortfalls associated with official crime statistics (although a low response rate of 60% was a problem). The *recorded crime* data, on the other hand, gives much fuller geographical coverage (the survey, for reasons of cost, could only be mounted in selected locations). It is thus rather more like a complete picture than a sample. This avoided the problem – an acute one for the survey – of not knowing in advance where local Safer Cities action would be sited. The recorded crime data has the further advantage of covering trends over a number of years rather than merely Before and After snapshots.

The structure of the report

Chapter 2 of this report presents the findings on Safer Cities impact on burglary from the survey, posing several fundamental questions. The first is 'Did the survey show a "Safer Cities effect" in terms of falls in burglary risk where action had been implemented?'. The risk does indeed fall, as shown by a simple comparison of changes in areas with and without action. The main task then becomes one of moving from this *prima facie* evidence to a conclusion that the Safer Cities action *caused* the fall, by eliminating several plausible alternative explanations. In this, we resort to statistical modelling techniques which seek to explain variations in burglary risk between individuals, and between areas, with reference to a range of extraneous influences. Having established with reasonable confidence that the falls in risk can be accredited to Safer Cities, we are able to pose the second and third fundamental questions, namely 'How great a reduction in risk did the burglary action achieve?', and 'What sort of money does one have to spend through Safer Cities action to prevent a burglary?'. In answering these questions, we examine evidence for side effects of action such as geographic displacement of burglary from the action area to elsewhere.

Chapter 3 presents the findings from the analysis of recorded crime, following the same sequence of questions. Again we resort to statistical modelling techniques to eliminate alternative explanations and to arrive at estimates of the reduction in burglary risk due to Safer Cities action, and of the cost of preventing a burglary. The results for the survey and the recorded crime analyses are for the most part remarkably similar. Chapter 4 reconciles the differences that do remain, before asking the key question 'Did the Safer Cities schemes offer value for money?'. This question focusses on the estimates of the financial costs of prevention set against the financial costs of burglary to victims and the State.

Chapter 5 returns to the survey to consider some of the less tangible consequences of Safer Cities action in terms of its impact on people's perceptions of their neighbourhood, and worry about burglary. It also examines the consequences for security-related behaviour, including membership of Neighbourhood Watch and the installation of home security measures. A paradox emerges between the evidence, on the one hand, that Safer Cities action reduced the risk of burglary, and on the other that respondents in the survey reported only limited awareness of action and no consistent change in security measures taken. In Chapter 6 we attempt to resolve this paradox with reference to measurement issues, and a discussion of the causal mechanisms by which the Safer Cities action had its impact on burglary risk. Chapter 7 raises further points of discussion.

To make for easier reading, major technical points are presented as end notes and appendices identified in the main text. Minor points are taken as footnotes.

2 The survey: evidence of impact on burglary

Over 7,500 interviews [end note 2] were conducted in 406 EDs. Two hundred and eighty of the EDs were located in 11 Safer Cities and the remaining 126 in eight comparison cities. The comparison cities were included to make sure that any apparent effect was not simply mirroring wider national trends. These cities were carefully matched demographically and on levels of recorded crime.[end note 3]

Half the interviews were conducted in September 1990, before much Safer Cities action had begun,[1] and half in September 1992, after a great deal had been implemented. To boost the sensitivity to change, as many of the *same* people as possible were interviewed in the two surveys – a so-called 'panel' survey. But to get sufficient numbers, other people were also interviewed.

To get round the difficulty of not knowing at the time of the 'Before' survey where local action would eventually be sited, we adopted a twofold strategy for choosing interview areas. Some of the EDs were selected as at high risk of crime and thus likely to be targeted by Safer Cities co-ordinators (the Census-based neighbourhood classification system known as ACORN was used for this purpose, calibrated against the three previous British Crime Survey sweeps — see end note 2). The remainder of the EDs were identified by co-ordinators themselves as being likely sites.

In the event, the strategy succeeded in obtaining a good-sized sample of local action despite its being widely scattered over each city. Of the 300 local schemes targetted on domestic burglary, 96 were covered. They fell in 117 of the surveyed EDs. (Some schemes covered more than one ED, and some EDs received more than one scheme.) The areas identified by the co-ordinators tended to have received quite large clusters of schemes, partly accounting for the overall high 'hit rate'.

---

1   Only a very small amount of action had been implemented in the surveyed EDs by the time of the Before–survey. It
     was judged unnecessary to take account of it in the analysis.

Local burglary schemes in the surveyed areas

The 96 burglary schemes covered in the surveyed areas are not very different from the full 300 local burglary schemes implemented through Safer Cities as a whole. Domestic target-hardening was by far the most common method in both cases, although the sampled schemes were somewhat more likely to involve community-oriented action. However, the sampled schemes had grants on average 44 per cent larger than domestic burglary schemes as a whole and covered areas 42 per cent larger. (This is probably because schemes covering larger areas had a higher chance of being hit by the survey; such schemes also tended to have larger grants.)

The amount of action present

In the 117 surveyed EDs in which there was Safer Cities burglary action, the amount (calculated as described) varied from 1p to £69 per household over the year preceding the After-survey.[end note 4] (Area scores of less than 1p per household were omitted.) The average amount was £11. A distinction was made between EDs in which under £1's worth of Safer Cities action was present per household over the year ('low' action); £1-£13 'medium' action; and over £13 'high' action areas. Of the 117 EDs with Safer Cities action, only 38 had any levered funds. The average additional levered input was £15 per household over the year. The levered funds are excluded from Tables 2.1 and 2.2 below, but are taken into account in the statistical analyses and cost estimation described later.

Changes in burglary risk:
did the survey show a Safer Cities effect?

We consider two measures of risk in the year prior to each wave of the survey. The first, a *prevalence risk,* measures what proportion of households said they were burgled at least once in the year of the survey. The second, an *incidence risk,* measures how many burglary incidents occurred per 100 households. In both cases, the offences considered are those where burglars got into homes—attempts are excluded.

Table 2.1 shows how risks of burglary *prevalence* changed between the 'Before' surveys, and the 'After' ones – in both the Safer Cities and the comparison cities.[end note 5] Before any Safer Cities action, burglary risks were somewhat higher in the comparison cities (12%) than in Safer Cities (10%), reflecting no more than inevitably imperfect matching. Between 1990 and 1992, burglary risks in the comparison cities rose by three per cent, well within the measurement error of the two surveys. The areas in the Safer Cities where there was no action on domestic burglary actually showed a bigger rise, of 15 per cent. However, in areas where there was action, risks fell by 10 per cent in the low-action areas, by 22 per cent in the medium-action areas and by 43 per cent in the high-action areas.

Table 2.1 Burglary prevalence: whether or not household burgled, by burglary action intensity

	Safer Cities					Comparison Cities
	Burglary action intensity score					
	none	low**	medium	high	all	none
		<£1	£1–£13	£13–£70		
Percentage households burgled one or more times in past year						
Before (1990)	8.9	10.3	12.7	13.4	10.2	12
After (1992)	10.2	9.3	9.9	7.6	9.6	12.4
percentage change (before to after)	**+15**	**-10**	**-22**	**-43**	**-6**	**+3**
No. of EDs	163	58	36	23	280	126
No. Schemes	0	34	40	41	96*	0
Weighted Data*** Unweighted No.	3,138	1,134	590	710	5,576	2,099

Source: 1990 and 1992 Safer Cities Surveys, SCP Management Information System, 1991 Census.

*   Number of schemes in cells sum to more than total due to some schemes covering EDs in more than one expenditure band.

**   The average expenditure per household in these bands is about 10p, £5 and £45 respectively. Scoring is explained in end notes 1 (general) and 4 (survey).

***   Weighting is explained in end note 5.

Table 2.2 presents similar findings for *incidence* risks, which give a better measure of the change in the number of burglaries (as opposed to the number of burgled households). Again, *the areas receiving the most action showed the greatest fall in risk.* However, in the case of the number of burglaries, there is an overall *fall* in *all* areas. This is the reverse of national trends as measured by burglaries recorded by the police in metropolitan forces, and by British Crime Survey trends between 1991 and 1993 in high crime-risk areas. An explanation most likely comes from the 'panel' respondents – householders interviewed in both surveys. We know from survey experience that, at a first interview, respondents are more likely to 'draw in' incidents which could have happened before the period being referred to, than they would in a second interview. While the fall common to all areas, then, may be explained by the panel component of the interviews, the *differential* fall in the action areas will not be. Moreover, it is possible to remove statistically the panel effect in estimating the outcome of Safer Cities action, and this is done later.

Table 2.2 Burglary incidence: burglaries per hundred households, by burglary action intensity

	Safer Cities					Comparison Cities
	Burglary action intensity score					
	none	low	medium	high	all	none
		<£1	£1–£13	£13–£70		
Burglaries per hundred households in area in past year						
Before	14.0	14.6	18.7	24.0	15.9	18.5
After	13.6	12.8	13.1	12.9	13.3	17.3
percentage change	**-3**	**-12**	**-30**	**-47**	**-17**	**-7**
No. of EDs	163	58	36	23	280	126
No. Schemes	0	34	40	41	96	0
Weighted Data Unweighted No.	3,138	1,134	590	710	5,576	2,099

Source: 1990 and 1992 Safer Cities Surveys, SCP Management Information System, 1991 Census.

See Table 2.1 for general explanatory notes.

There is a third measure of crime risk – *concentration*. This represents the number of burglaries *per victim,* and is a good indicator of repeat victimisation. (It is simply the ratio of incidence to prevalence.) We examined concentration to see whether there were any adverse side-effects of preventive action. In other words, it was possible that selective target-hardening of homes might lead to the offenders focussing all their efforts on the smaller pool of vulnerable homes that remained. There was no evidence that this had occurred, although the small numbers of repeatedly victimised households surveyed in some of the action bands made it difficult to discern reliable patterns.

From this simple tabular analysis of the survey data there is, then, *prima facie* evidence of a Safer Cities effect. Action against burglary in an area seems to produce a marked reduction in burglary risk. The effect moreover appears to be progressive: the more the action, the greater (and the clearer) the fall. Much of the analysis that follows seeks to test, develop and quantify this picture by considering plausible alternative explanations, which would account for the findings without recourse to the Safer Cities effect at all.[2] We begin by examining one particularly serious rival explanation that is clear even in the tables just presented, and then go on to a broader statistical analysis which takes account of a much wider range of factors associated with variation in burglary risk.

A first alternative explanation: selection effect?

One of the key features of Safer Cities was meant to be that high-crime areas were targetted for action. However, if co-ordinators targetted areas with *temporarily* extra-high crime levels, then a downturn in crime would be likely to follow whether or not the action itself worked. (This is known as 'regression-to-the-mean', or more strictly, the 'selection-regression artifact' [Campbell and Stanley, 1963; Cook and Campbell, 1979].) It would mimic a Safer Cities effect. As Table 2.2 shows, the prior burglary levels in Safer Cities EDs which received more action were indeed markedly higher than in EDs which received less action or no action – though they were not markedly higher than in the comparison cities. For example, high-action areas had an average incidence rate of 24 per 100 households per year, compared with about 15 in the Safer Cities no-action areas. The falls in incidence were all achieved by movements from the prior high to a common After-level risk of about 13 incidents per 100 households per year. On the face of it, then, the apparent Safer Cities effect might be explained away by regression-to-the-mean.

However, the tendency for more action to be focussed on areas with higher prior burglary risks can be seen from our detailed data to be rather a weak one, with much area-to-area variation beneath the overall pattern. Further evidence comes from a different source: the Safer Cities co-ordinators consistently stated in our interviews with them that where targetting of high-crime areas did occur, this was less on short-term 'blips', and more on the basis of 'bad area reputations' that were stable over time, and longer-term high rates of recorded crime. Moreover, the information base on which co-ordinators were able to pick targets was limited, and in many cases their ability to apply consistent 'rational' targetting, in the face of competing local pressures and demands, was constrained (Sutton, 1996). Tilley and Webb's (1994) closer study of ten Safer Cities burglary schemes reported that co-ordinators, while they targetted areas with serious burglary problems, did not always go for the very worst.

---

2   In case this is seen as unnecessarily 'unfair', it is worth noting that the process can serve equally to filter out the effects of factors which mask or distort the Safer Cities effect. Statistical testing was conducted on these subsequent, more sophisticated analyses.

These considerations notwithstanding, the only conclusive way of eliminating the regression-to-the-mean explanation would be to look at the burglary rate in the surveyed areas over a longer period. Did the areas which received action between 1990 and 1992 already have a persistent tendency to suffer more burglary, as the co-ordinators maintained? While the surveys can clearly throw no light on this question, the recorded crime data collected for the evaluation do.

The recorded crime data will be described more fully later, but for the present it is enough to note that data were available going back yearly from 1992 to 1987 for a large number of the surveyed EDs in the Safer Cities. Each surveyed ED was linked (using a geographic information system) to the police beat in which it was sited, and assigned the recorded crime rates of that beat, where and when available.[end note 6]

Figure 2.1 shows the *recorded burglary incidence rates* per household over the period 1987—90 for those surveyed EDs in the Safer Cities for which the recorded crime data was available. There are two sets: those EDs which received action scores, between 1990 and 1992, of £1 and over; and those receiving less than £1 or none at all. It also shows, for the same sets of EDs, the *burglary incidence rates from the survey* for the period 1990–92. Survey-based crime rates are always higher than the corresponding recorded crime rate due to non-reporting and non-recording. To simplify comparison therefore, the surveyed and recorded crime lines have been indexed at 100 to their respective absolute values in 1990. Were there to be a selection effect through regression-to-the-mean, the burglary rates in the selected areas would be higher than other areas only in the year or two prior to action, and before that would be closer to the rates in the areas which never received action. Figure 2.1 shows that this is not the case. The areas which subsequently received higher levels of action clearly did tend to have a consistent prior history of higher recorded burglary rates – indicating rather conclusively that *regression-to-the-mean cannot explain away the Safer Cities effect.*[3]

---

3   The pattern for the survey rates from 1990 to 1992 for this subset of EDs shows a similar pattern to the full set of EDs as in Figure 2.2. This tends to rule out distortion due to incomplete matching of EDs with recorded crime data.

Figure 2.1 Prior burglary rates of surveyed EDs indexed from 1990 £0–1 action

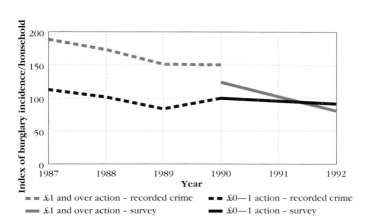

Statistical analysis: explaining variation in burglary victimisation risks

Although the regression to the mean possibility was ruled out, the patterns in Tables 2.1 and 2.2 still remain only *prima facie* evidence for Safer Cities impact on burglary, because they show the relationship between just three factors – time, location and action. There were other factors which were varying between the same places as the action and/or over the same time period. Any of these extraneous factors, alone or in combination, could have coincidentally accounted for the apparent Safer Cities effect. Alternatively, some may have worked in the opposite direction and caused us to *under*-estimate the effect. The main factors we considered were:

- features of *respondents* in the surveys, such as their age, class and whether they were new to the area (if, for example, we happened to interview more older people in the After-survey in the action areas, given that older people tend to be less at risk of burglary, this could have mimicked a Safer Cities effect; newcomers however tend to be more at risk (Foster and Hope, 1993), so an increase in the proportion of these would have masked a Safer Cities effect)

- features of the surveyed *EDs*, such as the level of deprivation or the number of young people (if some action areas contained more young people than others, this extra supply of potential offenders could have given them a higher risk of burglary; this would have introduced extra, unexplained background variation between action areas against which it would be harder for a Safer Cities effect to stand out)

- the presence of Safer Cities action *not* targetted on burglary

- demographic or economic features of the *city* level

- background trends in burglary at city and ED level

- a range of additional factors involved in the selection for the survey of
  the cities, EDs and the respondents living in them; the special effect
  of whether or not a respondent was a panel member was particularly
  important, as said.

The best way of getting beyond the *prima facie* results by filtering out any
influence of these extraneous factors is through multivariate analysis (or
'statistical modelling').[4] This examines the links between our measures of
outcome and Safer Cities action, whilst simultaneously taking account of as
many of the other factors as could also be measured. The analysis sought to
explain how the risk of burglary victimisation varied between individuals,
between the EDs covered and over time (before and after). This hierarchical
arrangement of our data required use of a relatively new technique, 'multi-
level modelling'. In constructing the models we used logistic regression to
explain the variation in risk of victimisation – for simplicity this required us
to focus on prevalence rather than incidence risks. Details are in Appendix 1.

The analysis moved in three stages. We took account first of the other
putative influences measured (reflecting the types of factors listed above,
and described in full in Appendix 1).

Second, given the large variation in burglary levels between EDs, and the
apparent siting of Safer Cities action in higher-risk areas, we also wanted to
take account of the extent to which an ED's *After* burglary risk could be
explained by its *Before* risk – for example, did EDs that had low burglary risk
in 1992 have similarly low risk back in 1990?[(end note 7)] In fact, the link was quite
strong, especially given the small numbers of interviews in each ED.
Incorporating it in the model enabled us to filter out quite a lot of otherwise
unexplained variation in EDs' After-risk – thereby making the detection of
Safer Cities effects easier. (Moreover, as will be seen, some Safer Cities
effects actually seemed to vary according to the prior burglary risk of the
area where the action was located.)

Third, measures of the Safer Cities burglary action were included in the
model to see whether, net of all the other explanatory factors included in
the statistical model, the action especially reduced the burglary risk in the
After-survey. This differential change in risk uniquely associated with the
presence of Safer Cities action, was deemed the Safer Cities effect.

---

4   Only to a very limited extent could these influences be filtered out by weighting tables (which was done).

The results of the analysis are best presented graphically. We begin with Figure 2.2, which shows the *observed* burglary prevalence rates, before and after Safer Cities action, for five sets of surveyed EDs. Reading from left to right, we have the EDs in the Comparison Cities; those in the Safer Cities with no action; those with low action; medium action; and high action. This is equivalent to Table 2.1, except that the burglary action in each set of EDs here is the *total* action recorded on the Management Information System – deriving from both Safer Cities funds and levered-in funds. (This – plus the absence of weighting, accounts for differences with Table 2.1.) Levered action was included both to get the clearest possible picture of cause and effect, and to enable investigation of the special effects of leverage.[5] Figure 2.2 shows the particularly large falls in burglary risk for the EDs with medium and high action. (It also shows the fact that these two sets of EDs had noticeably high prior burglary risks, as already discussed.) The statistical model developed to 'explain' the observed pattern of burglary prevalence is described more fully in Appendix 1. Overall, it proved to fit or 'predict' the observed data well.

Figure 2.2. Survey: before/after domestic burglary prevalence

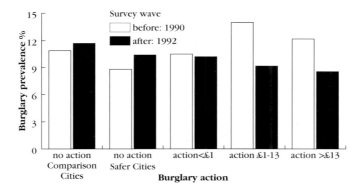

What part was played by the Safer Cities burglary action? Overall, net of all the other explanatory factors included in the analysis, *the occurrence of Safer Cities burglary action in an ED was followed by a reduction in risk in that ED, measured in the After-survey.* The effect remained when

5   The pattern is slightly different from that in Table 2.1, because a small number of EDs have been pushed up from low or medium action bands by inclusion of leverage, and because the weighting – used to get comparability between Safer Cities and Comparison Cities in the Tables – has been removed. The factors on which the weighting was done (the Local Authority District families used in selecting Comparison Cities, and the number of ED sampling points per city) were instead taken directly into account in the statistical modelling (as explanatory variables or in the hierarchical structure of the model itself).

estimated separately for panel and non-panel respondents, and for the areas identified for the survey by the co-ordinators versus those selected through ACORN.

The 'Safer Cities effect' appeared, at first sight, to be straightforward, with the greater the intensity of action, the greater the subsequent reduction in risk. (Typically, this is referred to as a 'dose-response' relationship.) But in fact it was not so simple, and there are several aspects of the relationship between burglary action and burglary outcome which should be described. First, we had to take account of any tendency for action to be *located* in areas with lower or higher than average risk, in order to reveal the changes *following* action. Second, unexpectedly, the mere presence of action in an area had a measurable 'step-down' effect on burglary risk independently of the intensity of the action (in fact, presence was a stronger and more reliable effect than intensity).[6] Third, neither the presence nor the intensity effects of action were constant: they altered in strength depending on the prior burglary level of the area in which the action was located.

Location of burglary action

- The action tended to be located in EDs which were at *higher* risk of burglary, confirming the earlier picture of co-ordinators' targeting strategies. However, relative to this targeting of areas with elevated risk, areas receiving *more* action tended to be those with *lower* risk. This is somewhat puzzling, but is at least consistent with findings from the interviews with co-ordinators (Sutton, 1996), which suggested that they often avoided areas with the very worst problems, for example because of a belief that schemes could not be given sufficient resources to make an impact there.

Changes in risk following the burglary action: 'step' and 'marginal intensity' effects

- The mere presence of action seemed to reduce the *after* risk of burglary quite markedly.[7] This will be referred to as the step effect of action.

- Additional to, and independent from the *step* effect, the *greater* the

---

6   The presence effect does not show clearly on Figure 2.2 or Table 2.1 (i.e., there is no marked drop in risk in the low action EDs). It only becomes apparent when extraneous influences are filtered out, in the modelling, and we move from comparing before and after risks, to comparing expected and observed after risks (Figure 2.3).

7   Statistically significant at p = .00006. Testing for statistical significance is described in Appendix 1.

intensity of action, the greater the reduction in the after risk. This will be described as the *marginal intensity* effect of action ('marginal' because we are talking about small, additional reductions associated with extra amounts of action in an area, on top of the original step down). It was not very reliable,[8] but worth noting (especially as the same is found with the recorded crime analysis that follows).

- The two effects together give a measure of the *overall* impact of the Safer Cities action. In simple terms, the overall impact in a locality is the sum of i) the step down in risk due to the mere presence of action, plus ii) the reduction at the margin due to the particular action dosage received there.

- Neither step nor marginal-intensity effects are constant, but vary with the prior burglary level of the ED where the action was located. The *step* effect appears to grow stronger, the higher the prior burglary level in an area.[9] This may reflect a *real* increase in strength. (It may be easier to reduce burglary in areas at higher risk, because offenders in such areas are not accustomed to much preventive action and respond more readily.) However, it may merely be a *measurement* phenomenon (it is harder to demonstrate reductions in risk in EDs whose burglary rates are already low to begin with – a 'floor' effect).[(end note 8)]

- The general marginal-intensity effect such as it is *fades out* in areas with higher burglary levels (it vanishes completely in areas with around 20% prevalence and above).[10]

The step effect was unexpected; but in following the logic of the modelling exercise, the empirical data 'out there' forced us to incorporate it in the course of explaining the observed variation in burglary risk.[11] As will be seen, the same effect was found with the recorded crime analysis. We discuss the implication of a step, or step-like, effect of the mere presence of burglary action in Chapter 6.

---

8 $p = 0.115$

9 The growth in the step is significant at $p = .0014$; the step and its growth are together significant at $p = 0.000002$.

10 The fading out tendency of the marginal–intensity effect is significant at $p = .016$; the marginal–intensity effect and its decline are together significant at 0.015. Interestingly, this is the opposite of what would be expected with regression-to-the-mean, if co-ordinators had been putting more funds into temporarily higher-crime areas. As will be seen below, the fading-out itself disappears when we focus solely on burglary action that is accompanied by Safer Cities action targetted on other crime types.

11 It is quite possible that the step is an over-simplification. For example the true picture could involve a very steep dose-response relationship when action intensity ranges from the minuscule to the merely very low, which *resembles* a step; the relationship may then tail off to form the gentle one, described above, as the marginal-intensity effect of action. Given the amount of variation between EDs in the size of the Safer Cities effect, it was difficult to discriminate such a possibility from a 'true' step. However, we did explore the step further by constructing a series of models where action present was simply represented as more or less than i) 10p; ii) 5p; and iii) 1p. Even in the last case, the presence of action at just 1p still produced a marked step down in risk.

Figures 2.3 and 2.4, which focus on burglary prevalence in the After-survey only, illustrate the findings from the statistical model. Figure 2.3 compares, for each of the familiar sets of surveyed EDs, what was *observed* in the After-survey with our best estimate of what we would have expected to have found in the same areas, had the Safer Cities action *not* been implemented, but all else had remained the same. (The method of doing this, 'sample enumeration', is described in Appendix 1.) From left to right, the EDs in the comparison cities and the Safer Cities with no burglary action both show the observed prevalence close to the expected. However, all three sets of EDs with Safer Cities burglary action show the observed prevalence in the After-survey to be markedly less than expected. The *step* effect is visible as this common drop.

Figure 2.3. Survey: expected & observed after, domestic burglary prevalence

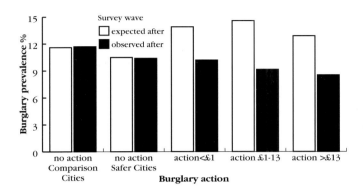

Figure 2.4.
Survey: relative percent change, domestic burglary prevalence

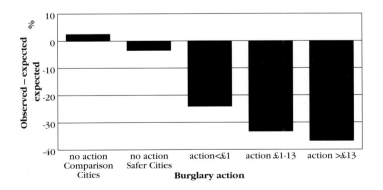

For comparative purposes it is better to look at the *proportional* reduction in burglary risk, by calculating the 'relative percentage change' (Ekblom and Pease, 1995). This is simply:

$$\frac{100 \text{ x (observed–expected prevalence)}}{\text{expected prevalence}}$$

Figure 2.4 shows the relative percentage change for the sets of surveyed EDs.[12] The comparison cities and the Safer City areas with no action are, again, close to expected. The action sets, though, show what appear to be both a common step down in risk to about 24 per cent below expected, and a marginal reduction on top of that as we go from low to medium (33% below expected), and medium to high action (37% below expected). These figures are specific to the sample of areas and individuals in the survey, and their influence on burglary risk. More direct estimates of the impact of action, which do not reflect the particulars of areas and individuals sampled (but derive straight from the regression coefficients in the statistical model), are presented subsequently.

Levered-in resources

The Safer Cities Programme is based in part on an 'investment' perspective so that for every pound's worth of improved locks, lighting, or support of Neighbourhood Watch spent by Safer Cities, it was hoped that there would be some levered-in resources (from, for example, other national inner-city programmes, local authorities, voluntary groups and individual domestic expenditure on security). Thus, these positive results need to be attributed not to Safer Cities' financial input *alone*, but to Safer Cities from its wider 'investment' perspective.

The question then arises as to whether the Safer Cities effect was any different in those areas where Safer Cities funds were specifically augmented by levered funds. Initial analysis suggested that action in such areas had a stronger effect (which might be consistent with schemes succeeding in obtaining levered funds if they were particularly well-planned or implemented). But further investigation revealed that this was due to the strong tendency for levered funds to be located in areas also receiving high amounts of Safer Cities money. When we conducted a special analysis of areas receiving high total action with and without leverage, there was very

---

12   The rpc was calculated separately for each *ED* (being our focal unit of analysis), and then averaged over the relevant set of EDs. It was not calculated from the average observed/average expected for each *set*.

little difference in the reduction in burglary risk.[13] (We should, however, note that co-ordinators felt that the levered-in resources were recorded rather intermittently on the Management Information System.) This suggests that levered money was as good as, but no better than, direct Safer Cities money in reducing burglary.

In sum, the statistical modelling has given us quite strong evidence for a step effect – the *mere presence* of Safer Cities action against burglary seemed enough to reduce burglary risk in the EDs where it was implemented. This effect appears to be stronger in areas where the initial risk of burglary is greater, although this may be a measurement artifact. There is weaker evidence for a further, marginal-intensity effect on top of the step. In other words, given that burglary action is present in an area, the *more resources* that it received, the *greater the reduction in risk.* However, this marginal-intensity effect diminishes in areas where the initial risk of burglary is greater. Whether or not some of the funds originated as leverage from other sources made no difference to the overall picture: the impact per pound was about the same irrespective of source.

Further alternative explanations?

On the face of it, this evidence for Safer Cities impact is extremely welcome. One major alternative explanation – regression-to-the-mean – has been ruled out along with other possible explanations based on socio-demographic differences between areas; but there are other possibilities which should be considered to *confirm* that the reductions in burglary risk are due to the Safer Cities burglary action. In particular, we have to examine the part played by *other* Safer Cities action not targetted on burglary; and action outside the Safer Cities Programme which may also have influenced crime disproportionally in the Safer Cities action areas.

The influence of other Safer Cities action

Burglary was not the only target of Safer Cities action. Schemes were implemented to tackle a range of other crime problems such as vandalism and disorder, and some schemes aimed to reduce the general propensity to offend. The presence of this 'other Safer Cities action' could well have

---

13 To anticipate the analysis of recorded crime data, the presence of levered funds again showed no extra impact there. In fact, in the police beats receiving Safer Cities action, the minority which also received levered funds (one in five of all beats receiving action), seemed to suffer an increase in risk. It is difficult to explain this, except to note that the beats with levered funds scored markedly worse in terms of their burglary risks in earlier years, and their index of deprivation.

affected burglary risks in the surveyed areas. We had already taken this other action into account in the statistical modelling in a simple way, including as an explanatory variable an action score based on the total financial input (both Safer Cities and levered funds) of all local schemes *except* those targetted on domestic burglary. Our estimates of the impact of burglary action were therefore *additional* to any effect on burglary of the other action. This model showed, unsurprisingly, that the other action tended to be located in areas with a lower burglary risk than the average in the surveyed areas. However, somewhat perplexingly, the burglary risk in the other-action areas *increased* in the After-survey. We therefore looked closer at the relationship between burglary action and other action.

Of the 280 surveyed EDs in the Safer Cities, 191 had some input of *other* Safer Cities action. About half of these EDs also had Safer Cities action against *burglary* while the remainder did not; the average amount of other action was the same in both cases, about £8.80 per household. Taking the other perspective, over three-quarters of the EDs with *burglary* action also received some *other* Safer Cities action. Those 25 which received burglary action *alone* had unusually high amounts of it (averaging £34.50 per household compared with £11.50 for the remainder). This was because a group of eight EDs with very high burglary action scores happened not to receive other action.

Given the strong tendency for Safer Cities burglary schemes to be located in areas which also had other Safer Cities action, it is important to investigate whether the impact of the former was gaining strength from the latter. If this were so, our estimates of the effectiveness of action targetted on burglary would be over-generous. We therefore extended the statistical model to explore how the effects of *burglary* action on burglary risk differed between EDs with, and without, other Safer Cities action. We simultaneously looked at the effects of the *other* action on burglary risk, with or without burglary action present.[14]

Altogether we compared three types of ED:

- *burglary plus other action together (96 EDs)*

- *burglary action alone (21 EDs)*

- *other Safer Cities action alone (95 EDs)*

---

14   The full set of permutations of burglary and other action, and their respective step and marginal–intensity effects, were included in the model; only a simplified account is given here.
We also examined whether there was any association between the presence of *levered* action against burglary, and the presence of *other* Safer Cities action. In fact, there was no link either way. With the EDs having *burglary* action, i) the proportion having *levered* funds was the same whether or not other Safer Cities action was present; and ii) the proportion having *other* action was the same whether or not levered burglary action was present.

Dividing the areas into these subsets considerably reduced the reliability of the findings, but with this caveat the more robust ones are worth reporting to help diagnose cause and effect.

With the areas receiving *burglary plus other action,* the effects of the *burglary* action are largely similar to those in the main model. (This is unsurprising because most of the burglary action was accompanied by other action, as said.) This applies to both step and marginal reductions in burglary risk. However, unlike the main model, the more *other* Safer Cities action in these areas, the further the burglary risk *fell.* In addition, the marginal-intensity effect of the amount of *burglary* action did *not* fade out in areas with higher burglary rates.

Interestingly, in contrast to the *general* relationship between burglary action and burglary risk, the presence of *burglary action alone* appeared not to reduce risk. The marginal-intensity effect of the *amount* of burglary action faded out when burglary levels exceeded the average.

The areas with *other action alone* again showed a weak tendency to have relatively lower than average burglary risk overall, as might be expected if co-ordinators were following sensible targeting strategies. Both the mere presence of the other action (i.e. other action's own step effect), and the amount (other action's own marginal-intensity effect), were markedly linked to an *increase* in burglary risk in the After-survey. Other action alone therefore appeared to increase burglary risk.

What can be made of these findings? First, it seems that *the impact of burglary action on burglary itself depends on the presence of other action in the same area.* The kind of burglary action implemented in Safer Cities may not work by itself, even though the amount of action in the 'burglary action alone' areas was in fact quite high. Those co-ordinators who introduced 'combined area safety packages' were exploiting this interdependence of impact. This dependence of the impact of burglary action on other action is particularly true of the (burglary action's) *step* effect, which *vanished* when other Safer Cities action was *absent.* It may help explain why the (burglary) step effect existed at all. After all, returning to our main model (which did not distinguish between burglary action alone versus with other action), it is puzzling to find that the mere presence of burglary action in an ED substantially reduced risk, even when the intensity of action was very small. It perhaps becomes less puzzling when we realise that low burglary action EDs, whilst receiving an average of only 11p of *burglary* action per household, were also receiving some £5.30 input of *other* action. On average in the areas where both types of action were present, for every pound spent on burglary action, something like 75p per household was spent on other action. This cross-subsidy from other action has obvious cost-effectiveness implications, although it may have had additional benefits in preventing other crimes.

Second, *the marginal-intensity effect of burglary action may be more robust when it is accompanied by other action.*

Third, there may be evidence of 'inward' crime switch: *the presence of other action alone in an area may increase the risk of burglary by causing offenders to switch from other crimes to burgling homes.*

Fourth, *there may be a kind of 'protective' effect of burglary action:* in areas where other action is accompanied by burglary action, there is *no* evidence of crime switch into burglary. Indeed, there may be a *synergy* – perhaps one that is necessary for the burglary action to work at all.

These observations, whilst interesting, must for the moment remain at the more speculative end of our conclusions. This is partly due to statistical unreliability, and partly because a more thorough investigation would require looking in more detail at the specific types of other action present. We will, however, briefly return to the question when analysing the recorded crime data below.

The influence of action outside the Safer Cities Programme

The Safer Cities Programme did not exist in isolation. Urban areas with multiple problems received a great deal of remedial action – social, economic and architectural. The aim of Action for Cities (of which Safer Cities was one element) was to achieve co-ordination of local initiatives. Some of this other action is likely to have influenced burglary risks. Its effects could, therefore, be confused with those of Safer Cities schemes targetted on burglary. If there was any tendency for Safer Cities co-ordinators to direct their schemes towards areas in receipt of extraneous action, then this could have boosted the measured impact of the Safer Cities schemes as a whole. Unfortunately, we could not measure such other action directly (it would have been a further major undertaking), so it cannot be ruled out as a factor in the results. But overall, our interviews with co-ordinators revealed they had no consistent tendency to site, or to avoid siting, schemes where extraneous action was present (Sutton, 1996). The co-ordinators, in deciding where to locate action, had to respond to a variety of policy considerations, and experienced a variety of constraints.

Specifically on Safer Cities *burglary schemes* though, Tilley and Webb (1994) noted a tendency for co-ordinators to avoid targetting areas where it was thought that other major efforts might be made independently of Safer

Cities. In particular there was some concern to avoid jeopardising future Estates Action bids (illustrating the complex financial and political context in which the 'rational' preventive process had to operate; see also Sutton (1996)). If Safer Cities burglary action was systematically directed away from such major extraneous inputs, then this would in general understate our estimates of impact.[15]

We have so far considered a number of alternative explanations for the apparent Safer Cities effect – regression-to-the-mean, independent differences in associated factors, especially sociodemographic ones, the role of other Safer Cities action, and the role of extraneous action. Overall, while some uncertainties must remain, these have not detracted from the view that the Safer Cities action against burglary caused the reductions in risk we observed. We can now go on to estimate the size and cost of the Safer Cities effect.

Some cost–effectiveness considerations from the survey findings

Cost-effectiveness assessments are notoriously difficult, and the ones here are no exception. Nonetheless, one fair question to ask is: 'How great a reduction in risk did the burglary action achieve?'. Another is 'What sort of money does one have to spend to prevent one burglary?'.

How great a reduction in risk did the burglary action achieve?

The statistical analysis showed that the link between input of Safer Cities funds, and outcome in terms of a reduction in burglary risk, was not straightforward. The mere presence of Safer Cities action against burglary reduced risk and beyond this, risk progressively diminished even further with increasing intensity of action. These effects were both modified by the prior burglary risk in the area where the action was located. There are grounds, too, for thinking that the effect of the mere presence of burglary gained some of its strength from the presence of other Safer Cities action in the area.

From the model of burglary risk which we constructed in the statistical analysis, we were able to produce numerical estimates of the overall and marginal impact of action. (Full details of calculations are in Appendix 1.) It is important to remember that the estimates relate to the impact of action on *all households in an area* – it is impossible from our data to estimate the

---

15   This is because the extraneous action would tend to have its impact on burglary in areas within Safer Cities which received no Safer Cities action – including the relevant EDs in our evaluation. If there were a greater tendency for burglary risk to be reduced in such areas, the *differential* reduction measured in the Safer Cities action EDs would be less, as it would be measured relative to these extraneous EDs.

impact of a certain sum spent on *individual households*. It should also be borne in mind that these are direct estimates of impact in the kinds of areas we sampled, deriving from the relevant regression coefficients in the statistical model. Unlike the reductions in risk shown in Figures 2.3 and 2.4, they are not specific to the composition of areas and individuals in our sample, so direct comparisons cannot be made with these.[16]

We look first at the main model, which made no distinction between burglary action with, and without, any other Safer Cities action. At the average (prior) burglary prevalence of 10 per cent, the best estimate of the *step* effect of burglary action is that it reduced burglary risks by 29 per cent. In other words, *the mere presence of Safer Cities action against burglary seemed to reduce the risk of burglary by over a quarter.* On the *marginal-intensity* impact, given the presence of action, *for every additional pound of action per household the risk of burglary fell by a further 0.1 per cent.* Step and marginal-intensity effects combined showed an *overall* reduction of 31 per cent for an area with average action intensity.

At a prevalence risk of a little over 20 per cent, the marginal-intensity effect drops out altogether, and in fact thereafter is linked to a *rise* in risk, which is difficult to interpret. However, as said, there were indications that this fade-out was confined to circumstances where burglary action was implemented *alone*, in the absence of other Safer Cities action. The impact on risk in the majority of burglary action covered by the survey, which was accompanied by other Safer Cities action, is somewhat different. The step effect is rather less than its counterpart in the main model (16% as opposed to 29%); the marginal-intensity effect is rather more (0.57% per £1 of action, as opposed to 0.1%), and it continues to exist at very high levels of risk. However, these estimates are less reliable.

What sort of money does one have to spend to prevent a burglary?

We converted the estimates of burglary risk reduction into estimates of the average amount that one would need to spend, on local action of the kind and quality implemented in Safer Cities, to prevent one burglary incident. (Calculations are in Appendix 1.) There are two types of cost estimate that are of interest to decision-makers concerned with implementation of cost-effective preventive action. *Overall cost* is the cost of preventing one burglary, taking all the Safer Cities effects into account – both the presence of burglary action and the amount. This figure informs the decision *'is this preventive action worth implementing at all?'* *Marginal cost* is of interest

---

16   Nor can they be directly compared with Table 2.1 because this shows before to after drops in risk rather than observed versus expected risks in the After-survey.

when the first decision has already been taken. It is the cost of preventing *one more burglary* through extra action. This figure informs the decision *'given that we have already decided to set up some preventive action, how much should we implement in the target area?'*. All other things being equal, the marginal cost of preventing one more burglary is likely to be greater than the overall cost, because it ignores the effects of the mere presence of action.

Both Safer Cities scheme expenditure and leverage are included in our cost estimates. Local and central administrative costs over the lifetime of the Programme were also taken into account (adding 50p overhead to every £1 spent on scheme funding). We allowed, too, for repeat victimisation: according to our survey, every burglary *victim* prevented meant an average of 1.5 fewer burglary *incidents*. (This ratio was surprisingly constant over the range of prevalence covered by our surveyed EDs.) Finally, we assumed that any effect of Safer Cities action would endure for two years. This assumption in particular is returned to in the discussion.

Overall costs

It was not straightforward to calculate the cost estimates from the values obtained in the statistical model and our other cost figures just described. We costed the step at the *average* input intensity of £16.[17] Since there was some evidence that the step effect gained strength from the presence of *other* Safer Cities action, it is reasonable to add the average amount of other action[18] – namely £7. (The other action, may, of course, reduce other types of crime risk – but this cannot be estimated.) In total, the average input associated with the presence of Safer Cities burglary action plus other supporting action was taken to be £23.

Marginal costs

The marginal cost is, as said, how much *more* money needed to be invested in an area, at the time the action was originally implemented, to prevent *one more burglary*. The marginal cost of preventing one extra burglary was estimated in a similar way to the overall cost, with one additional stage. The calculation (see Appendix 1) involved comparing the estimated overall effect on risk of £16-worth of action (the average intensity) and £17-worth. This put a figure on the reduction

---

17   This is because with step effect, cost literally did not come into the statistical relationship, it being the mere presence of action which appeared to have an impact. Taken to an extreme, this could produce estimates of cost effectiveness ranging from infinite to infinitesimal – we would expect an almost 30% fall in action whether £1,000 was spent in an area, or a fraction of a penny! Instead of the average intensity, one might have wanted to use the lowest possible intensity of action that produced the step reduction in risk. However, as described already, even a penny per household (the minimum intensity we incorporated in the analysis) seemed to show a substantial reduction.

18   More precisely, the average amount of other action present in areas which also received burglary action.

in risk associated with an extra pound's worth of action per household.

This produced the figures below. They are taken from the estimated effects of burglary action in the presence of other Safer Cities action, which comprised nearly three-quarters of the action EDs.

- Where risks are *very high* – where householders have a 20 per cent chance of being a victim of burglary with entry in a year[19] – the cost of preventing one burglary is estimated to be about £200 overall, and £900 at the margin. In other words, if a co-ordinator spends £200 in an area with this risk, this will, on average, prevent *one* burglary in a two-year period. However, if the co-ordinator wants to prevent *two* burglaries, the cost will be £200 + £900 = £1,100.

- Where risks are *high* (from a national perspective, but average in our survey) – in an area where householders have a 10 per cent chance of having a burglar in the home in a year – the cost of preventing one burglary is estimated to be about *£400* overall, and *£1,500* at the margin.

- For those in areas with a *nationally average* risk of a burglary with entry of three per cent (according to British Crime Survey estimates), the Safer Cities cost of preventing a burglary may be a little over *£1,400* overall, and about *£4,800* at the margin. However, this takes us beyond the kinds of areas we surveyed.

The figures above take account of levered funds. If these are excluded in favour of an 'investment' perspective, the costs in terms of purely Safer Cities money are almost a third lower.

The figures for both overall and marginal costs show that when burglaries are common, it needs *less* expenditure in an area to prevent them than when burglaries are *rare*. This is consistent with common sense – more relief can be obtained, for example, from hardening targets under constant attack than from hardening targets that are rarely the subject of burglars' attention. The main source of this relationship is simply the fact that the preventive action is achieving a *proportional* reduction in risk. A risk reduction of a fifth in an area suffering from a risk rate of *six* per cent prevents twice as many burglaries for the money spent in the area, as the same one-fifth reduction in an area with the same number of households but a risk rate of only *three* per cent.

---

19 This level of risk was found or exceeded in 71 of the 406 EDs we surveyed. However, sampling error from the small numbers of interviews in each ED made the ED risk levels fairly unreliable.

Did the *proportional* reduction in risk achieved by Safer Cities action itself change with the burglary risk in an area? Prior burglary risk was taken explicitly into account in the statistical model, but as already described had a rather complex influence on the impact of action, depending on whether or not the burglary action was accompanied by other Safer Cities action. As we calculate using a progressively higher prior burglary rate (right-hand column of Table A1.4, Appendix 1), the *overall* proportional reduction in risk associated with preventive action remains roughly constant (for all burglary action) or even shows a slight decline (for 'accompanied' burglary action). All this suggests that while preventive action may be better *value for money* where burglary risk is high, proportionally speaking it achieves no greater reduction in *risk*.

Some costing issues

It is important to note some technical restrictions in the meaning of these costs derived from our analysis:

- The marginal cost refers only to the effects of extra action put in place as part of the original scheme – for example, a scheme which covered more homes than initially contemplated. Fresh action, whether a second wave of the same kind of preventive measure, or the implementation of a different method altogether, could well have 'reinvigorating' effects of its own. However, this was not studied.

- Our marginal cost estimates do not directly inform the decisions *'how large an area (or how many homes) to cover?'* and *'how much money to spend in absolute terms?'* – they only relate to increases in the intensity of action in a given target area. Economies of scale may be achieved, but on the other hand some larger schemes may be less thoroughly implemented. Our evaluation does not cover these aspects.

- While we refer to the overall and marginal costs of preventing one or one more burglary, it is worth re-iterating that our estimates relate to area average costs and do not directly inform the decision *'how much money shall we invest in protecting this particular home?'* Our costs have no direct implications for single-household strategies such as targeting repeat victims (Farrell and Pease, 1994; Farrell, 1995), except to note that these should not neglect exploiting area effects. Since repeat victimisation may account for a greater proportion of all crime in areas with higher crime risk (Trickett et al., 1992), targeting repeat victim households and targeting high crime areas may naturally go together.

The estimated costs of prevention are indicative rather than precise. The statistical 'margins of error' were very broad,[20] and to have reduced them noticeably would have involved inordinate expenditure on more interviews. Due to the nature of the mathematical relationships in the model, the estimate of the cost at the margin in particular was not robust,[21] and for reasons explained in Chapter 4 the marginal cost estimate from the recorded crime analysis is to be preferred. There are two additional reasons for the imprecision. First, costing typically involves making assumptions, and this was the case here too. Second, there is some uncertainty about trends in the Safer Cities areas which received no action, an issue which raises the possibility of displacement to these areas. We consider these issues in turn.

For our cost-effectiveness calculations, we assumed the following:

- A scheme's impact will last for two years, as said, reflecting current understanding that preventive measures may have only a limited span of effectiveness. While this seems reasonable and conservative, reliable quantitative evidence to support it is lacking.

- The action score an area received was not systematically affected by co-ordinators' directing further funds into existing success stories, which would exaggerate our estimate of impact (Mark, 1983). Nor, conversely, was it affected by their sending good funds after bad, in an attempt to resuscitate failures (Skogan, 1990) which would contribute to an understatement of impact. Interviews with co-ordinators suggested neither tendency operated overall.

- On average, there was no tendency for Safer Cities action to be located in the same places as other local action–outside the Safer Cities Programme – on crime and social problems more generally, which would give our estimates an unfair boost. Although we could not measure this directly, interviews with co-ordinators again suggested no such tendency overall.

- In estimating the size of impact of Safer Cities action it was reasonable to take account of the *rise* in burglary risk in the Safer Cities EDs where there was no action. This is discussed below.

Integral to the calculations of prevention costs were the figures for how

---

20   The terms representing the Safer Cities effect in the statistical analysis, while significantly improving the fit of the model to the observed data, nevertheless had wide standard errors. This is unsurprising given the range of schemes covered by the model, and their diverse local circumstances.

21   Using bigger margins, such as an extra £10 worth of action, gave cost estimates over a third cheaper than the ones presented, which were based on a margin of an extra £1.

burglary changed where there was *no* Safer Cities action. As shown in Table 2.1, there was a 15 per cent increase in the prevalence risk of burglary in the Safer Cities EDs receiving no action, as against a mere three per cent rise in the comparison cities. These respective figures partly determine our estimate of the size of the Safer Cities effect. This is because, in the statistical analysis, the differential fall in burglary risk in the action areas was estimated *relative* to the rises elsewhere (i.e. Safer Cities no action areas, and comparison city areas). These were the best indication of what would have happened had there been no action. If we discount the big increase in risk in the Safer Cities no-action areas, this would considerably increase the estimates of the costs of preventing a burglary. It is therefore important to consider what might lie behind this increase. One possibility is that the increase in risk simply reflected a greater overall increase in crime in the cities in the Safer Cities Programme relative to the comparison cities. (As already said, Safer Cities action was too modest to have a measurable impact on crime city-wide.) This is borne out by recorded crime statistics at least, which show that the domestic burglary rate for the Safer Cities rose by 30 per cent between 1990–1992, while comparison cities rose by only 20 per cent. This supports the idea of a 'real' increase, and argues against the cost estimates having been set too low. Displacement – another possibility – is more problematic.

Geographic displacement

On the face of it, the marked increase in prevalence risks in the no-action areas in Safer Cities (Table 2.1) suggests that the burglary prevention efforts in action areas may have caused offenders to turn their attention to the no-action areas. The possibility of geographic displacement must be considered, then, even though the general criminological evidence for its importance and pervasiveness is not strong (Barr and Pease, 1990, 1992; Hesseling, 1994), and it is very difficult to assess in any evaluation (Ekblom and Pease, 1995). Given the importance of displacement both as a process in its own right, and as a potential obscuring factor in our main impact assessment, we made several attempts to explore it, each more strenuous than the last. In the end, we did find evidence for displacement, but only under certain conditions.

It is possible to explain away the *prima facie* evidence for geographical displacement in the survey findings. The increase in burglary risk in the surveyed *no-action* areas can be seen as no more than a manifestation of a 'background' increase in recorded crime risks in the Safer Cities as a whole. There is also the fact that the increase in risks seems simply too large to be entirely accounted for by displacement from the action areas surveyed. (By definition, the increase in the number of burglaries due to displacement *per se* can never exceed the fall in the action areas.) Moreover, many of the action areas will be quite some distance from the areas where there is no action in the same city. Bear in mind here that there is plenty of evidence from other studies that offenders usually operate locally (Davidson, 1984; Maguire, 1982).

These points aside, displacement may still have occurred. There were, for example, some indications of it in a number of the Safer Cities burglary schemes studied by Tilley and Webb (1994), and it is important to try to assess it using other, more direct approaches. We therefore tried to take account of any burglary action in the *ring* of EDs that surrounded each surveyed ED in the Safer Cities (the *'bullseye'* – see Table 2.3). This was 'extra' action only; it excluded schemes which covered both the surrounding neighbourhood and the surveyed ED itself.[22] Three 'extra adjacent action' scores were generated for each surveyed ED, to explore close-range and somewhat longer-range effects: i) burglary action in the *inner ring* of EDs immediately adjacent to the bullseye; ii) burglary action in an *outer ring* of EDs immediately outside the inner ring; and iii) a pooled score of burglary action anywhere in *either or both inner and outer rings*.

We then distinguished between our surveyed EDs on the basis of whether or not they had burglary action in the bullseye, and whether or not they had extra burglary action in the various surrounding rings. There were seven distinct geographical patterns:

> (a) Action in *bullseye* alone
>
> (b) Action in *bullseye* and extra action in *inner ring* only
>
> (c) Action in *bullseye* and extra action in *outer ring* only
>
> (d) Action in *bullseye* and extra action in *both rings*
>
> (e) No action in bullseye but extra action in *inner ring* only
>
> (f) No action in bullseye but extra action in *outer ring* only
>
> (g) No action in bullseye but extra action in *both rings*

Of the 280 surveyed EDs in the Safer Cities, 109 had extra burglary action in one or other or both of their surrounding rings. About half of these 109 also had action themselves, i.e. in the bullseye. The respective 'extra, adjacent action' scores were incorporated in slightly simplified versions of the existing statistical model.

---

22   We reasoned that schemes which covered ring(s) and bullseye together would not shift crime from one to the other.

The results of this analysis were complex, and technical problems make it difficult to estimate the statistical significance,[23] so they must be used as diagnostic clues rather than firm findings. (A fuller account is in Appendix 2.) Nonetheless they are extremely interesting. They can be understood in terms of three additional processes: *displacement, diffusion of benefit, deflection* (and a broader process of *'security enveloping')*[24] plus the preventive 'Safer Cities effect'.

Table 2.3 presents, for each of the seven geographical patterns, the amounts of various kinds of *action present in the bullseye and rings,* and the *changes in burglary risk in the bullseye* that are associated with the action.[25] As with the main analysis, we have to distinguish between the effects of the *presence* of action (in the bullseye and/or in the relevant ring) and the marginal-intensity effects of the *amount* (again, in the bullseye and/or in the relevant ring). In some circumstances the amount and the presence of action exert *opposing* influences on risk. In the description that follows, it should be borne in mind that the results for the action in the bullseye and inner ring only – the second column in Table 2.3 – are particularly unreliable given that they are based on only three EDs.

---

23   In many cases, particularly in the smaller cities and boroughs surveyed, the bullseye of one surveyed ED also comprised part of the ring of another. This means that the assumption of independence of the areas sampled is violated. This may be connected with the observation that incorporating 'extra adjacent action' scores in the statistical models in most cases actually worsens the fit slightly.

24   Additional, more speculative, process are discussed in Appendix 2.

25   The change in risk in the bullseye was the effect of action in the bullseye itself, plus any *inward* displacement or diffusion of benefit from action in the surrounding rings. We were unable to measure risk in the rings themselves, to look at *outward* displacement from the bullseye, because the rings themselves were not consistently surveyed. This made it impossible to estimate the *balance* between basic reduction of burglary achieved in the intended action area on the one hand, and displacement and/or diffusion of benefit *from the same action* to the environs.

Table 2.3 Survey – evidence of displacement and other geographical processes

	Action **present** in bullseye and extra action:				Action **absent** in bullseye and extra action:		
	Nowhere else	Inner ring only✠	Outer ring only	Both rings	Inner ring only	Outer ring only	Both rings
Surveyed EDs:	67	3	19	28	22	22	15
EFFECTS	EVIDENCE OF IMPACT ON BURGLARY RISK‡ IN BULLSEYE						
Prevention	Step & Marginal decrease in risk						
Displacement					Step increase in risk in absence of action in bullseye		
Deflection/ Security enveloping		Step decrease in risk when action in both bullseye and ring(s) ? Marginal decrease in risk when action in both bullseye and ring(s)					
Diffusion of Benefit					Marginal decrease in risk in absence of action in bullseye		

‡ Risk is the odds of burglary victimisation (prevalence) in each surveyed ED; change in risk is the percentage reduction in the odds of victimisation specific to the after survey, associated with presence and/or amount of the relevant type/s of action. Numerical estimates are in the 'components' rows of Table A2.1 in Appendix 2.

✠ Since there are only 3 EDs in this set, the results are particularly unreliable although they are mostly consistent with the pattern in the other sets; the large marginal increase in risk per £1 extra in the ring may be attributed to sampling error and/or the very high amount of action in the inner ring coupled with low burglary and other action in the bullseye.

? Indicates a contrary result, although unreliable.

Displacement seems to appear where there is no action in the bullseye. The *step* effects of adjacent action show a clear *increase* in risk in the bullseye when extra action is present close by. However, this is not the whole story, because the marginal-intensity effects operate in the reverse direction. The increase in risk due to the *presence* of adjacent action is progressively *eroded,* as the intensity of adjacent action becomes higher. It is possible that two processes are occurring. First, offenders may be relocating their efforts in the light of knowledge that 'something has been done to enhance household security' in their favoured area. This may merely drive them to the immediately adjacent streets. Second, higher intensities of action may put them off altogether, especially if they are unsure of the boundaries of the action. Given that they may be unwilling to travel greater distances and/or to unfamiliar territory (Brantingham and Brantingham, 1991), this may have served to produce a real drop in offending. Since this relative reduction in risk appears to cover an area wider than the intended area of the scheme, the marginal falls may be evidence for *diffusion of benefit* (Clarke and Weisburd, 1994). There is no reason why a single scheme could not have both displacement and diffusion effects simultaneously: diffusion in its immediate vicinity, displacement further away.

Deflection is the keeping of crime away from an area (cf Barr and Pease, 1990). In our survey, deflection seems to appear when there is action in the bullseye and the rings together. Under these conditions, the extra adjacent action *reduces* the risk in the bullseye.[26] This is true for both presence and amount of adjacent action. What seems to be happening is that under the joint influence of action in the rings and in the bullseye, offenders are inhibited, or displaced elsewhere. (We cannot tell which, from our data, so cannot claim this as evidence of 'absolute' protection against displacement, i.e. a fall in the total amount of burglary measured over a wide area.) Action in the bullseye therefore seems to be protecting it from inward displacement from neighbouring schemes. The different burglary schemes located in the ring and the bullseye in effect may link up to provide one common area which is unattractive to burglars. This could be called *'security enveloping'.*

Prevention. The EDs with action in the *bullseye* but *no extra adjacent action* show the Safer Cities effect: the usual pattern of reductions of risk associated with the presence and the amount of action. The step effect for these 67 EDs is weaker than the overall step effect for all 117 EDs with

---

26 This was with the partial exception of the marginal–intensity effect of action in the inner ring only. There were only three surveyed EDs with bullseye action, plus extra action in the inner ring only. This renders these results particularly unreliable. The high amount of extra adjacent action, together with the unusually low amounts of burglary action and other action in the bullseye may also have been responsible for the extreme and sometimes anomalous effects displayed.

action (9% reduction in odds of victimisation versus 25% in the main model, not shown in Table 2.3). This suggests that the step effect in our main model was boosted by adjacent action deflecting burglary further away – the 'security enveloping' already mentioned.[27]

So far, we have considered these component influences individually. When we add their effects, the burglary action in the bullseye and the extra adjacent action in the rings work together to reduce the risk in the bullseye, often to a substantial degree. For example, in the 28 EDs with action in the bullseye and extra action in both rings, the overall reduction in risk is in the range 60–70% (depending on the amount of action in each). When there is no action in the bullseye, the *direction* of the effect of extra adjacent action depends on its *intensity*. With *low* amounts of adjacent action, its step effect prevails and there is an overall *increase* in risk in the bullseye (for example, an almost 70% increase in risk with £1 of extra action in the rings). With *moderate-to-high* amounts of extra adjacent action, by contrast, the marginal-intensity effect prevails and there is an overall *decrease* in risk in the bullseye (for example, a *decrease* in risk of nearly 80%). In these circumstances, the more intense action may have driven offenders further off, caused them to switch to other targets, or forced them to give up altogether. From the statistical model, the threshold for a net decrease in risk in the bullseye is about £4 of action per household in the rings.

We have thus tentatively identified a menagerie of effects of adjacent action – displacement, deflection, security enveloping and diffusion of benefit. All of these predominate under different conditions. What clearly emerges is that a position of 'blanket pessimism' – a reluctance to implement situational prevention on the grounds that its benefit is inevitably neutralised by displacement – is untenable.

Ideally, one would want to use the quantitative estimates of the net changes in risk that seemed due to displacement or diffusion of benefit, in correcting the costing of preventive action (to be assessed in Chapter 4). But this would have had to rely on too many untested assumptions about (for example) how rapidly the *real* effects tail off with distance. It would also have ignored possible reductions in the sensitivity of *measurement* of effects at greater distances. It would have been jumping too far ahead of the data in a very complex and rather speculative analysis. This, together with the difficulty of significance testing already described, means that for the moment, it is perhaps most sensible to be neutral about the effects of displacement on cost.

---

27   Indeed, this also links up with the fact that the Safer Cities effect was stronger in those surveyed areas identified by the co-ordinators where concerted action was implemented.

Can we say that some types of action worked better than others?

Most of the burglary *schemes* involved 'target hardening', as described in Chapter 1. However, schemes were often combined in a locality, with other (generally community-oriented) action against burglary, and/or action against other crimes. Of the 117 *areas* with burglary action covered by the surveys, a third had target hardening alone; similar proportions had other *burglary* action alone, and combined action. As already described, four-fifths of the *burglary* areas also had Safer Cities action targetted on *other* crimes, or crimes in general. (This pattern was consistent across the three types of burglary action area already described.)

Disentangling the different contributions to the reduction in burglary was difficult, especially since burglary action areas without additional action against other crimes were rare, and since co-ordinators reported directing other burglary action to areas which had already received target hardening from other sources. Our findings – from the surveys[28] - are tentative as we were at the limit of the resolvability of reliable patterns in the data.

We constructed an extended statistical model which separately represented areas with different combinations of action (although to simplify analysis we merely included the presence of each combination, and omitted intensity). We covered the following mutually exclusive sets of areas:

- target-hardening burglary action + other burglary action + action against other crimes (31 EDs)

- target-hardening burglary action + other burglary action (7 EDs)

- target-hardening burglary action + action against other crimes (31 EDs)

- other burglary action + action against other crimes (34 EDs)

- target-hardening burglary action (7 EDs)

- other burglary action (7EDs)

- action against other crimes (95 EDs).

---

28   It was even more difficult to disentangle the effects of different types of action with the recorded crime analysis that follows, because the larger size of the areas studied (beats rather than EDs) made for more overlap between measures of action for different schemes.

The combination with the strongest and most reliable effect on burglary was when all elements were present. Target-hardening reduced burglary under all conditions in which it was present. Purely community-oriented burglary action, however, only worked in tandem with action against other crimes; where it stood alone there was no reduction in risk, although there were only a few areas in which this condition was met.

Our earlier analysis showed that when burglary action was considered as a whole, the support of action against other crimes seemed more generally important. Like other studies, then (Tilley and Webb, 1994; Osborn and Shaftoe, 1995), this evaluation suggests a comprehensive approach is best, although target-hardening could work alone.

Summary

To sum up the results of the survey analysis, we have shown good evidence of Safer Cities impact on domestic burglary. This evidence remains after eliminating a number of alternative explanations for the reduction in risk. The presence of action in a locality is followed by a reduction in risk of the order of 30 per cent, a result which may depend in part on the presence of Safer Cities action targeted on *other* offences. Burglary action itself seemed to be more effective when a variety of methods were employed in an area, not just 'pure' target-hardening. Other types of action against burglary – particularly 'community-oriented' action–especially needed shoring up by action against other offences. There are limited indications of a further decrease in risk with greater amounts of action. Evidence for both geographical displacement and – under more restricted conditions – diffusion of benefit was also found. The presence of burglary action in an area seemed to protect against displacement of burglary from burglary action in neighbouring areas. It also seemed to protect against offenders' 'crime switching' into burglary, when other crimes were targetted in the same area.

3 The recorded crime statistics: Safer Cities impact on burglary

Outcome data

We collected recorded crime data for up to 12 major offence categories, including domestic burglary, from 14 of the 16 Safer Cities evaluated (there were problems with data supply in the other two, Wandsworth and Islington). Our aim was to get annual totals for each offence, from 1987, the year before the Safer Cities Programme began, to 1992. Ideally, we planned to obtain these figures for every beat.[1] In practice, this proved to be impossible.

- Some data were missing for certain years, or certain beats.

- Some offence categories were aggregated inconsistently between police forces (although this was not a problem with domestic burglary).

- Some beat boundaries were changed.

The last problem was resolved by looking back through past maps to uncover 'beat pedigrees', and identify 'superbeats' – groups of adjacent beats whose common outer boundary remained about the same despite changes within. With this, we arrived at a 'standard beat map' for each city which covered the whole time period. (Gaining continuity was therefore achieved at the cost of increased 'graininess' of the picture in some places.) In this way, we achieved full geographical coverage in 13 of the Safer Cities for which crime data was available, and partial coverage in Birmingham.

Altogether in 14 Safer Cities, we obtained data for 701 beats or superbeats.[2] Ideally, over the six years studied, this would have yielded (701 x 6 =) 4,206

---

1   We chose the smaller area if records were available for both foot and vehicle beat.

2   Superbeats comprised 12% of the total number of areas; about a third of the total number of households.

'beat-years' (i.e., one incidence risk measurement for each beat in each year). In practice, for the reasons stated above, we actually obtained data for only 3,277 beat-years. However, for almost 60 per cent of beats we had measures for all six years.

There was considerable inconsistency between and even within police forces in terms of whether or not attempted burglaries were included in the counts they supplied, or pooled with other categories such as criminal damage. We had no alternative but to ignore the distinction. For our outcome measure we needed to convert the burglary counts into *incidence rates* per household. For this, the standard beat maps were 'digitised' and merged with population data from the 1991 Census on a geographic information system. In effect, each beat was 'tiled' with the Census data from the EDs which most closely approximated its territory. This process also enabled us to link to the beats contextual data from the Census and its derivatives (such as the Index of Local Conditions, which is a set of measures of deprivation (DOE 1995)). The beats varied widely in size and population, with averages of 230 hectares and over 2,200 households.[3] They were thus on average about ten times the area and the population of the EDs used in the survey.

Comparison outcome data took two forms. As with the survey, we compared beats receiving Safer Cities action at some point over the six year period (mostly towards the end) with those which did not. We also looked at a set of nine carefully-matched *comparison cities* to provide a picture of more general national trends in similar urban areas, over the six years. These cities were matched to Safer Cities equivalents by four *'family groups'* taken from Craig's (1985) classification of local authority districts based on the 1981 Census, as with the survey. They were also selected for comparability of total recorded crime rates over the period 1986–90.

To reduce cost and effort, we did not collect beat-level data for the comparison cities. Instead, we used their *city-level* annual figures to construct two 'indicators' of crime rates. A *global* indicator was based on all comparison cities, with burglary incidence risk weighted to adjust the population composition by family group, in the comparison cities, to the composition in the Safer Cities. There was, however, considerable variation in crime trends observed between the family groups. Therefore, a *family* indicator was calculated separately for each family group of Safer Cities, based on the appropriate comparison cities.[(end note 9)]

---

3 'True' beats averaged 180 hectares and 1,700 households; superbeats 600 hectares and 6,300 households. Unless otherwise specified, all further references to beats include superbeats.

The amount of action present

Burglary schemes

As with the survey, we identified the local Safer Cities schemes targetted on domestic burglary which were in the right time and place to link up with our outcome measures. We succeeded in covering 240 schemes out of the total of 300 current or completed by Summer 1992.

Units of analysis: action beats and action beat-years

Almost half of the beats (325/701) had burglary action at some point. These measures of *place,* we call *'action beats'.* We calculated the burglary action score as the average input of Safer Cities funds per household in the relevant beat and over the year in question. While the scores in the survey had a once-only value (i.e., for 1992, the year of the After-survey), the scores for the recorded crime analysis were calculated separately for each beat-year in which there was action. These we call *'action beat-years'.* They are measures of both *time and place.* In a few cases, beats had action scores from 1989 onwards, although the bulk of the action was implemented over 1990–1992.[4]

Altogether out of the 3,277 beat-years for which we had recorded crime data, 734 – about one in five – had some action. The average action intensity in each of these action beat-years was just over £2.50 per household from *Safer Cities* funds. *Levered* funds were also present for 149 action beat-years, the average intensity being £5. Average *total* intensity, combining Safer Cities and levered money, was £3.57 per household. Table 3.1 summarises the available units of measurement for crime and action data.

---

4   The scoring for the survey simply assumed that once started (in 1990 onwards for the relevant Safer Cities) a scheme's action continued to exert any effect at least until the After-survey in 1992. With the scores for the recorded crime, to make the time factor as similar as possible, we assumed that once a scheme had started, its influence would continue to be felt for a two-year period. In practice this meant that virtually all schemes covered were still contributing to the action score in the last year, 1992.

Table 3.1: Units of measurement for the recorded crime analysis

Unit of measurement for burglary and burglary action	Unit with burglary action present
Beat 701	**Action beat** (action present in beat in at least 1/6 years) 325 (average total action intensity £4.50 in 1992)
Beat–year (701 beats, for up to 6 years each) 3,277	**Action beat–year** (action present in this beat, in this year) 734 (average total action intensity £3.57 over all years)

In the *final year of measurement,* 1992, there were 325 action beats. The average intensity from Safer Cities funds was £3 per household. Eighty-two of these beats also had *levered* funds, an average score of nearly £5.50 per household. The *total* score was nearly £4.50.[5] For purposes of presentation, we divided the beats into sets on the basis of the total action present in the final year.[6] There were (i) 375 beats which *never* had action; (ii) 266 which ended up in 1992 with under £5-worth of action per household (average just under 50p); (iii) 26 with action between £5–£13 (average nearly £8); and (iv) 33 with action over £13 (average £34). Figure 3.1 shows, for these sets of low, medium and high action beats, the time course of action over the years 1987–92. The action in each set starts to appear between 1989–90, and reaches highest levels in 1992.[7]

---

5   These scores were smaller than their equivalents for the surveyed EDs, because the larger area of the beat meant that a scheme might only cover a small part of it.

6   This was almost always the maximum action score received over the six year measurement span. The bands were selected to occupy distinctively different parts of the range, and give reasonable numbers of beats and beat-years per set whilst being as close as possible to those in the survey presentation.

7   Because our scoring calculation system had been set to assume that action, once started, continued to exert its effects for two years, the 1992 scores were in effect cumulative for virtually all action, since the bulk of it started from 1990 on.

Figure 3.1 Crime: Burglary action scores by year

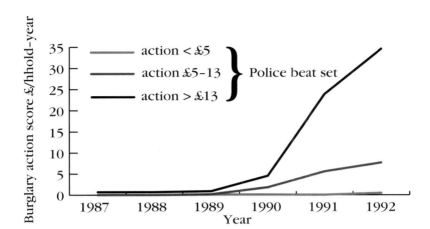

As with the survey, there was an association between levered funds and high amounts of Safer Cities action. The 82 action beats with levered funds had an average of just over £7.50 Safer Cities burglary action per household in 1992; the 243 without leverage, just over £1.50. Of the 33 beats in the high (total) action set, 22 had leverage.

Changes in burglary risk: did the recorded crime data show a Safer Cities effect?

The recorded crime outcome measure is an *incidence* rate – the number of domestic burglaries per 100 households in each beat, in each year.[8] Figure 3.2 shows the average incidence rates for the low, middle and high sets of action beats, as they changed over time. It also presents the same burglary trends for two other series: the 375 beats with no burglary action, and the global comparison indicator, a weighted aggregate of the nine matched comparison cities.

---

8   As said, an indeterminate number of these may have been attempts.

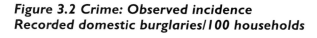

Figure 3.2 Crime: Observed incidence
Recorded domestic burglaries/100 households

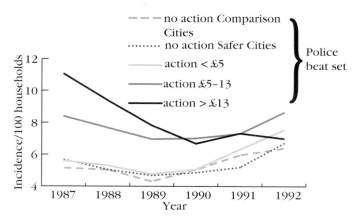

Several things are apparent from Figure 3.2. First, there is a trough in each series at about 1989 or 1990, corresponding to a trough in national crime rates at the time. Second, as with the survey, the middle and high action sets start off with markedly higher risks of burglary. Third, while all other series continue to rise through to 1992, the high-action set alone shows a return to a falling trend. This pattern does therefore show some *prima facie* evidence of a Safer Cities effect, but this is confined to the high-action set. There is, moreover, a possibility that the final fall is no more than a resumption of the earlier one.

Statistical analysis: explaining variation in burglary incidence risks

Once again, to clarify the picture we needed to turn to statistical modelling. This attempted to explore the link between the presence of Safer Cities action in any one beat in any one year, and the domestic burglary incidence risk.[9] More specifically, we sought to estimate how far the presence, and the amount of Safer Cities action explained the observed variation in the burglary risk in the Safer City beats, net of other factors which might also have influenced crime. The 'other factors' we were able to include in the analysis were more limited than for the survey. They are summarised below, and listed in full in Appendix 3. The *survey* included coverage of inhabitants of comparison cities, and its statistical model attempted to explain variations in burglary risk in both Safer Cities and comparison cities together. The *recorded crime* model merely attempted to explain the variation in burglary risk in the Safer Cities beats alone, using the comparison indicators as additional *explanatory* factors.

---

9   Burglary *incidence* risk was used here, in contrast to the prevalence analysis with the survey data, because prevalence data was not available from police records. Since areas were the fundamental geographical unit of analysis here, not individual households, there were no difficulties in analysing incidence. The incidence risks were heavily skewed towards zero, so an appropriate transform was found in the *arcsine of the 4th root* of the risk rate. This greatly reduced skewness, but some curtosis remained.

The statistical model was again hierarchical: up to six years' data per beat, and an average of 50 beats per Safer City. At the *city* level, the other factors in the model included:

- demographic data from the Index of Urban Conditions (such as indices of overcrowding, mortality, long-term unemployment)

- the 1981 Census 'family type' of the relevant local authority district (since we had 'stratified' the sample of comparison cities using this).

At the *beat* level:

- geographical factors such as the size of the beat, the household density, whether it had a city-centre location (since domestic burglary rates are likely to differ in areas comprising mostly shops, offices, transport and entertainment facilities)

- social factors derived directly from the 1991 Census, such as the proportion of the population aged 16–24, the proportion aged 60 and over, and the proportion of households lacking a car. Other factors from the Index of Urban Conditions were also included, such as the overall Index itself, and subsidiary indicators including overcrowding, and children in unacceptable accommodation

- measurement factors which could have introduced bias – whether or not a 'beat' was a superbeat; and whether or not we had obtained burglary data in the beat for all six years ('incomplete' beats may have been areas with special problems or unusual patterns of policing).

At the *beat-year* level:

- the year (to indicate the overall trend in burglary)

- comparison indicators for burglary, both global and based on city Census-family

- the amount of *other* Safer Cities action, not targetted on burglary, that was present.

Representing the Safer Cities action in the statistical model

As with the survey, to arrive at an estimate of any reduction in burglary risk that followed implementation of Safer Cities action, we had also to take account of the effect of where the action was *located*. For example, co-ordinators could have selected beats for action which tended to have a *faster decline in burglary* over the *whole* period of measurement, not just following the implementation of Safer Cities action. Failure to filter this out could have mimicked any Safer Cities effect. Figure 3.2 shows some evidence for this confounding possibility.

In the statistical model, we took account of each action beat's *average burglary risk* over the whole six-year period.[10] To filter out any locational effects which changed over time, we first took account of the *overall burglary trend* over time in the action beats. However, using this simple time trend was not enough, because, as Figure 3.2 makes clear, burglary rates were not behaving in a consistent way over time (i.e., rising over the whole period 1987–92, or falling over the whole period). In most of the Safer Cities beat sets, and in the comparison cities, burglary rates fell to about 1990, and then rose. In order to reflect this U-shaped pattern, we took account of any special year-by-year relationship between burglary risk in the action beats and the patterns shown by the appropriate *comparison city indicators*.

Results

The simple plot of burglary risk over time has already provided an indication of a Safer Cities effect, in the beats receiving a high intensity of action (Figure 3.2). Results from the statistical modelling[11] confirm this and further support the findings from the survey. *Net of all the other explanatory factors included in the analysis, Safer Cities action in a beat, in a given year, was associated with a reduction in risk.* Again, the mere presence of the action on a particular beat-year, and the intensity of that action, showed independently measurable reductions in risk.[12] These are the details, taking first the locational effects of action, and then the ('true') Safer Cities effects:

Location of burglary action

- Action tended to be located in beats with *higher* risk of burglary, when averaged over the whole six-year period; but (as with the surveyed EDs) among these action beats, it was the ones with *relatively lower* risk that received the more intense action.

---

10 Or the average risk over a lesser period, if six years' worth of data were not available for a given beat.

11 Appendix 3 shows the full model, which contained a large number of terms whose purpose was to remove the static and dynamic locational effects of action. These were not included in an attempt to 'flush out' an elusive Safer Cities effect; the effect in fact was rather obvious from the simplest models, and the terms were introduced to try to 'shoot it down' by alternative explanations. In most cases, the inclusion of locational terms trimmed rather than enhanced the estimated size of the effect.

12 It was difficult to take explicit account of the 'prior burglary risk' as the survey did, for two reasons: i) this was a time series rather than before and after, with action starting, in a beat, during one of several different years; and ii) some action beats did not have the full series of observations back to 1987. These both meant that a common 'prior year' could not be identified.

- Action tended to be located in beats showing an overall background *decline in burglary risk* over time. The intensity of action showed a similar relationship, albeit small in magnitude. If they had not been taken into account, these combined locational effects would have led to an overestimation of the Safer Cities effect.

- The location of action showed a rather more complex pattern relative to *the national trough in burglary* (around 1990) represented by the comparison indicators, which was difficult to interpret.[13]

Changes in risk following the burglary action

- Net of the locational effects of burglary action, and all other factors taken account of in the model, the mere *presence of action* in a given beat-year seemed to reduce the risk of burglary markedly.[14] This is the step effect.

- Beyond and above the step effect, the greater the intensity of action, the greater the reduction in risk. This was only 'borderline' significant,[15] as was the similar finding from the survey. But given the similar direction, it is more reasonable to accept rather than reject it.

Figures 3.3 and 3.4 illustrate these findings from the statistical model. Figure 3.3 shows the risks of burglary incidence *expected* in the low-, middle- and high-action beats, had no action taken place. (The estimation process is described in Appendix 3.) It successfully reflects the high burglary risk in the early years in the middle- and high-action beats, and their steeper decline. (This shows that the statistical model has taken account of these locational trends and will not confuse them with the Safer Cities effect.) *After* the dip, all beat sets are expected to rise. This is in line with the observed trend in the comparison cities and the Safer Cities beats with no action. However, the expected rise is particularly marked in the high action beats.

---

13   The action tended to occur in beat-years which were lower in risk relative to the global comparison indicator applied to all Safer Cities, but higher in risk relative to the indicator linked to the Census family group of the particular Safer City. Greater intensities of action were associated with an increase in risk with the global indicator, but a decrease with the family indicator.

14   Statistically significant at p = 0.027.

15   p = 0.108. The step and marginal-intensity effects taken together are jointly significant at p = 0.01.

Figure 3.3 Crime: expected incidence
Recorded domestic burglaries/100 households

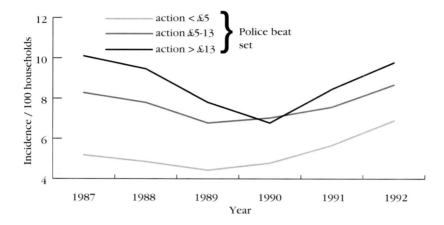

Figure 10 presents the differences between observed and expected, as a *proportion* of the expected risk level–the relative percentage difference.[16] Up to 1990, this figure remains close to zero and fairly flat for each beat set, indicating again that the beats with action were displaying trends that were expected on the basis of all the extraneous factors taken into account. In 1991, however, all three sets show marked dips (ranging from 10-20% below expected). The only ones to continue below expected in 1992, though, are the medium (4% below expected) and high action beats (30% below, continuing on down). This suggests that the effects of action of lesser intensity in a beat may be rather more short-lived.

---

16   Relative percent *difference* is used here in preference to the relative percent *change* used for the survey, because there is a series rather than a simple before–after comparison.

Figure 3.4 Crime: Relative percentage difference Recorded domestic burglaries/100 households

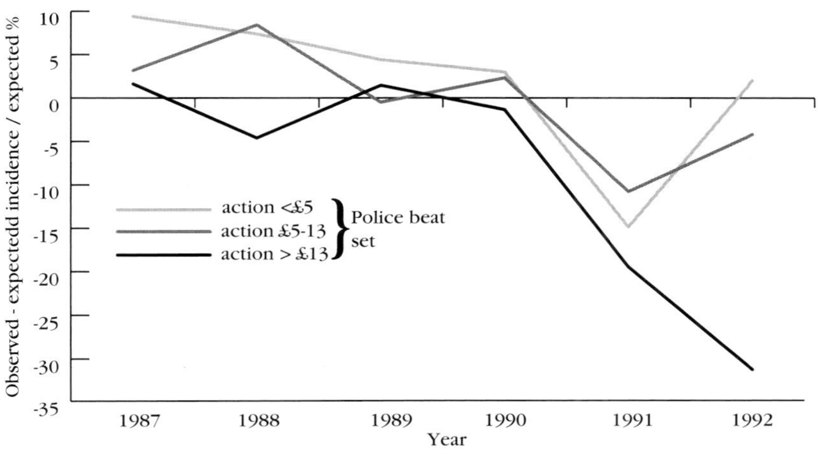

The role of other Safer Cities action

As with the survey, our analysis of recorded burglary incidence attempted to take account of the presence of other local Safer Cities action. A score for 'all local action' was produced, and the burglary action score subtracted from it. This 'other action' score was included in the main statistical model. It shows that the intensity of other Safer Cities action was associated with an independent, additional, drop in risk. However, it was hard to disentangle the effects of other Safer Cities action from those of burglary action, because over 90 per cent of beat-years with burglary action also had other action present.[17] Only 10/734 beat-years with burglary action occurred in beats which never received any other Safer Cities action over the six-year period. Despite this unpromising overlap, we did try to explore the contribution other action made to the estimated impact of burglary schemes, given its significance in the survey results. The results were, indeed, unclear, but they did confirm the survey finding that where other action was present but burglary action was absent, there seemed to be an *increase* in risk of burglary (albeit a not very reliable one). This suggested that the other action may have led to a crime switch into burglary, fended off by the presence of burglary action.

---

17   The average score for the other action was £7.73 on the 685 beat-years where burglary action was also present; £6.23 on the 825 beat-years without burglary action.

In sum, we have shown some fairly strong evidence from the analysis of the recorded crime data that a Safer Cities effect occurred. Burglary risk was reduced when action against burglary was present; the reduction was stronger with more intense action, although as with the survey this was not very reliable. Beats with higher-intensity action seemed to show more lasting reductions in risk, although evidence was limited.

In reaching our overall conclusion, we have sought to filter out alternative explanations based on the locational effects of action: that action might have tended to be sited in beats which were low in risk anyway; and/or declining in risk anyway. The effect does depend on the assumption that action beats would, in the absence of Safer Cities burglary schemes, have followed the dip and rise found elsewhere – namely, in the no-action beats and in the comparison cities. However, this seems reasonable. Given the presence of other Safer Cities action in most of the beat-years when burglary action occurred, it also seems reasonable to make the conservative assumption that this other action contributed to the observed impact on burglary.

On this basis, we can produce estimates of the size of the Safer Cities effect from the recorded crime analysis, to set alongside those from the survey.

Some cost-effectiveness considerations from the recorded crime findings

Estimating cost effectiveness from the statistical model of the recorded crime data followed similar lines to the procedure for the survey estimates. We begin by presenting a general estimate of the size of the reduction in risk associated with Safer Cities action, and then go on to produce costings. Details of calculations and assumptions are in Appendix 3.

How great a reduction in risk did the burglary action achieve?

At a 10 per cent incidence level of risk (equivalent to the average prevalence risk in the survey) *the mere presence of Safer Cities burglary action seemed to reduce the risk of burglary by about seven per cent.* On the marginal impact, *given the presence of action at the average intensity* (£3.57 per household), *for an additional £1 of action the risk of burglary fell by a further 0.8 per cent.* Step and marginal-intensity effects combined showed an *overall reduction of some ten per cent* at the average action intensity.

What sort of money does one have to spend to prevent a burglary?

We converted these figures into the average amount that one would need to spend, on local action of the kind and quality implemented in Safer Cities, to prevent one burglary incident. The procedure was very similar to that used for the survey cost estimates, and used the same cost figures and assumptions. We costed the step effect at the average action input of £3.57 per household. Since we again had to take account of other Safer Cities action, we costed this at the average input of £7.73. In total, the average input associated with the presence of Safer Cities burglary action, plus other supporting action, was £11.30 per household. This included levered funds.

- Where risks are *very high* – where there are 20 *recorded* burglary incidents per hundred households in a year (equivalent to 30 *'real'* incidents per hundred households, and a prevalence risk of 20% as measured by the survey) – the Safer Cities overall cost of preventing one ('real') burglary is estimated to be about £360, and the marginal cost £1,300.

- Where risks are *high*–in an area where there are 10 recorded burglary incidents per hundred households in a year (equivalent to the average prevalence risk of 10% in the survey)–the overall cost of preventing one burglary is estimated to be about £550, and the marginal cost a little over £2,000.

- For those in areas with a risk of three recorded incidents per hundred households in a year – equivalent to the *nationally average* prevalence risk from the British Crime Survey, of three per cent – the overall cost of preventing a burglary is estimated at a little over £1,400, and the marginal cost about £4,700.

The figures for both overall and marginal costs show that when burglaries are common, it needs less expenditure in an area to prevent them than when burglaries are rare. Again, as with the survey, the main source of this relationship is the fact that the preventive action is achieving a *proportional* reduction in risk.

These findings are a powerful argument for targetting action on very high-crime areas, other things being equal. Identifying these areas of extreme risk (which are usually very localised) appeared to be difficult for the co-ordinators or the police to do themselves (Sutton, 1996). For the future, progress is most likely to be made through developing postcode-level computerised databases to carry several years-worth of crime data (to guard against unquestioning targetting of meaningless 'blips'), and appropriate retrieval and analysis systems.

Did burglars switch to other property crimes?

We have already shown that preventive action against *other* crime problems may increase the risk of burglary, unless there is 'protection' from burglary action in the area. But did the burglary action itself cause offenders to switch to other crimes?

To explore this possibility we looked at what happened, in the burglary action beats, to the risk of *other* property crimes, of the kind which frustrated burglars might be expected to turn to. Robbery and theft from the person, as 'contact' crimes, were left out as we felt these involved a marked shift in offending style. We produced a combined risk rate (in each beat-year)[18] for :

- other burglary (mainly commercial)

- theft of vehicle

- theft from vehicle

- theft from shops

- other theft.

We constructed a statistical model very similar to the one for explaining variation in risk of domestic burglary – but this time, of course, the variation explained was in risk of other property crime. We also included indicators of other property crime from the comparison cities.[19] We then included all the other explanatory factors we had used in the domestic burglary model, including the entire set of burglary action terms – both locational effects of action and 'Safer Cities' effects.

If burglary action caused a crime switch, then we would expect the risk of other property crime (as measured) to increase following the burglary action's implementation. In fact, we did find a slight increase, of *5.3 per cent* in the risk of other property crime associated with the mere presence of

---

18   The combined risk-rate was simply the sum of individual offence risk rates. Since some of these were per capita, and others (e.g., theft of car) were per car-owning household, the number, while useful for present purposes, had limited meaning.

19   We again had to transform the outcome measure (and the comparison indicators), to render it approximately normal. However, the risk exceeded one in some beats, because it was the sum of area aggregate risks from several crime types. Therefore we could not use the arcsine (4th root) transform, but had simply to use a 4th root transform instead. The transformed data appeared reasonably normal.

burglary action.[20] However, this was counteracted by the effects of the intensity of burglary action. Above an intensity of almost £5 per household of burglary action, there was a net *negative* effect on risk. In other words, a small amount of burglary action may induce burglars to switch to other property crime in the locality, but a moderate to large amount of burglary action seems to help protect against other property crime. This finding was net of the effect of other Safer Cities action (some of which could be expected to influence the other property crime directly – in fact, the presence of other action itself independently reduced the risk of other property crime a little further).

---

20   This was calculated at the average composite risk of other property crime.

4 Were the Safer Cities burglary schemes value for money?

From the survey and the recorded crime statistics, we now have two independent estimates of the reduction of burglary risk associated with Safer Cities action against domestic burglary. We also have two sets of estimates of what it cost, under various conditions, to prevent a burglary through Safer Cities action. Here, in Chapter 4, we contrast our estimates of the direct financial cost of prevention with the costs of burglary itself, to victims and the State. We first do this separately for the survey and recorded crime estimates. We then try to reconcile the differences, to arrive at an overall conclusion about direct and quantifiable value for money. In Chapter 5, we assess some non-financial effects of Safer Cities burglary action.

Although our methods have taken us much further than other programme evaluations in assessing whether the preventive action was good value for money, we still cannot answer this with complete confidence. This is because of the inevitably complex problems discussed above in assessing the costs of preventing a burglary in Safer Cities action areas, and of knowing *for certain* whether the reduction in risk observed was *entirely* due to Safer Cities. There is also the uncertainty of knowing how much crime in the action areas was displaced elsewhere. If one allows, conservatively, for the possibility of *some* displacement, then the cost estimates would obviously be higher than we have given, because some of the apparent local reduction in risk is shifted elsewhere into higher risks for others. By the same token, if diffusion of benefit extended the effects of higher-intensity burglary schemes beyond their intended (and funded) boundaries, then our cost estimates would be too high. Evidence for both displacement and diffusion was found under different conditions in the survey analysis (it was not possible to do this for the recorded crime in the time available), and the conclusion there was that the most sensible position to adopt for costing was a neutral one.

Value for money: the survey estimates

1992 BCS figures indicate that burglaries excluding attempts, on average, cost victims living in the same kinds of areas as those sampled for Safer Cities about £900 gross.[1] (About £400 of this, on average, is recouped through insurance – though this does not take away the cost, but merely redistributes it, socially, in terms of the cost of insurance premiums.) A current Home Office estimate of the cost of a domestic burglary to the Criminal Justice System – for the police, courts and prisons, etc. – is about £300. (This takes account of the fact that not all the burglaries that occur are recorded and thus incur CJS costs. It ignores any area differences – costs in high-crime areas may differ, but this cannot be estimated.) All told, then, from the crime survey perspective an average burglary in the sort of high-crime area we are considering carries a financial cost of about £1,200.

In areas of *high* burglary risk (EDs with 10% prevalence), our estimate of the *overall* costs of preventing a burglary amounts to about £400, with levered-in funds, administrative costs and expenditure on other Safer Cities action taken into account (Appendix 1). Here, typical Safer Cities burglary action – in the presence of Safer Cities action against other crimes – would easily pay its way in financial terms alone. The marginal cost of burglary action was only £1,500 per burglary prevented – in the same region as the cost of burglary.

Value for money: the recorded crime estimates

The closest we could match the areas covered in our recorded crime data to British Crime Survey areas was through the category 'Inner City', used in sampling local authority districts in the BCS (SCPR, 1993).[2] We used the estimated cost to victims in these areas, giving a figure of about £800, a little less than that used for the survey costing. Costs to the state were again taken to be £300. The total financial cost of a recorded burglary to victim and state is therefore £1,100.[3]

In areas of *high* burglary risk (ten recorded incidents per hundred households), our estimate of the *overall* costs of preventing a burglary

---

1   The costs per burglary incident (whether or not recorded, but excluding attempts) included loss due to stolen property and damage, and time off work. The figures were produced using the same 1981 ACORN categories that the survey sample of EDs was drawn from. In these areas, the costs are noticeably lower than the 1992 BCS national average of £1,378. The current (1994) national average estimate is £1,600.

2   Costs to victim households reporting their burglaries to police in 'Metropolitan' areas – also used as a category in BCS – were considerably higher, at about £2,000.

3   We did not use the victim costs per *reported* burglary (slightly larger, at over £900); nor did we adjust up the costs to the state to take account of the fact that *all* recorded crimes would incur state costs. This was to maintain equivalence of costs between survey and recorded crime estimates, by focusing in each case on costs of 'real' incidents rather than just recorded incidents. However, the cost per *real* burglary incident is plotted against the incidence of *recorded* burglary in Figure 4.1b. Since the recorded crime data did not consistently distinguish between burglary with entry and attempts – which would cost less – our cost of burglary figure is probably a few percentage points too high.

amounts to £550, with levered-in funds and administrative costs taken into account. This time, the *marginal* cost is a little over £2,000. From the recorded crime analysis, typical Safer Cities burglary action would easily pay its way in overall terms, but would be somewhat high in marginal terms.

Value for money: a final view

As local burglary risk increases from 'nationally average' to 'very high', the *overall* cost of preventing a real burglary drops from £1,400 to £200 from the survey (with other Safer Cities action present); and from nearly £1,000 to £300 from the recorded crime. The equivalent marginal estimates range from £4,800 to £900 for the survey, and from £4,700 to £1,300 for the recorded crime. Figures 4.1a and 4.1b illustrate these ranges. Given the differences in the data and the statistical models used (discussed in Appendix 4), these are remarkably close and well within any latitude of error. Their similarity gives confidence in their reliability.

Figures 4.1 Cost-effectiveness estimates – burglary
Results from survey

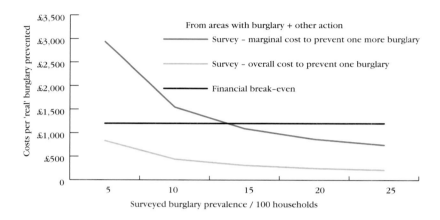

Figure 4.2 Cost-effectiveness estimates – burglary
Results from police recorded crime

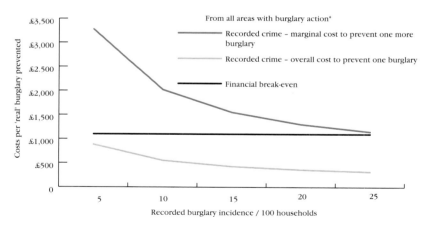

* Nearly all these areas also contained other action

Crime switch

There was some evidence of crime switch *to* burglary when Safer Cities action not targetted on burglary was implemented in the absence of burglary action. But crime switch *from* burglary to other property crimes seemed only to occur at low intensities of burglary action – there was some reduction in the other property crimes at higher intensity (over £5/household). Taking a conservative view, we should continue to regard the current cost estimates as gross *local* estimates – i.e., applying to the gains in the action areas only. However, we should also take note of the indication that diffusion of benefit may have outweighed geographic displacement and crime switch in areas with more intense burglary action.

This means that we can conclude that on the financial balance sheet, the Safer Cities action against domestic burglary was cost-effective. Our conclusion is based on a comparison between gross estimates of the immediate costs of prevention and the financial costs of burglary itself, but took some account of unintended effects such as displacement or diffusion of benefit. It applied both to the overall cost, and under higher-crime conditions typical of cities, to the marginal cost. Taking account of any *non-financial* benefits of action, such as the avoidance of misery, upset and worry suffered by burglary victims and fellow residents, would make for an even more favourable picture. Current Home Office costing takes £600 as a measure of this upset – which would place even the recorded crime estimates of the marginal cost below the cost of burglary, in areas of higher risk. Some further non-financial effects of Safer Cities are explored in Chapter 5.

Total gains from Safer Cities domestic burglary prevention

It is possible to take the cost-effectiveness calculations a further step, albeit with wide margins of error, to estimate the total gains from the Safer Cities Programme's domestic burglary prevention schemes. A fuller account is in Appendix 3.

From the recorded crime model, the estimated cost of preventing a burglary through Safer Cities action – at a typical 'city-level' risk of 10 incidents/100 households – is £552. Of this sum, a large element derived from 'other' Safer Cities action not targeted at burglary, and from overheads. The direct (Safer Cities and levered) cost through funding of anti-burglary action was £116.

Assuming leverage on the full 500 anti-burglary schemes to be in the same ratio to Safer Cities funds as the leverage on the 300 for which we have data, we calculate that some £6.6 million funds, both Safer Cities and levered, were directly spent on anti-domestic burglary action. Dividing this figure by £116, the direct cost of preventing a burglary through funding of anti-burglary action, produces an estimate of over *56,000 burglaries prevented.*

If each burglary prevented had a total (direct and indirect) cost of prevention of £552, and avoided a cost to victims and the state of £1,100, then it represented a *saving of £548.*

Multiplying this saving by 56,000 burglaries prevented gives a rough estimate of *£31million saved by the £4 million (plus £2.6m leverage) spent on local Safer Cities domestic burglary schemes.* Displacement may have negated some of this gain, but as said elsewhere, it is likely that in many circumstances this was countered by diffusion of benefit. Although there are very wide margins of error, it appears that the financial preventive savings from the burglary schemes alone may have virtually paid for the entire Phase 1 Safer Cities Programme.

5 Impact on crime prevention behaviour and worry about burglary

The survey enabled us to look for evidence of the impact of Safer Cities burglary schemes on a wider range of outcome measures. These included behavioural measures (membership of Neighbourhood Watch and domestic security levels) and perceptual measures (people's worry about burglary and their perceptions of the local area).

Neighbourhood Watch

Only one scheme in the surveyed EDs where action was located explicitly set out to establish Neighbourhood Watch (through the employment of a community worker), although nine others also employed 'outreach workers' or sought to raise the profile of community safety through publicity. However, Table 5.1 shows that membership of Neighbourhood Watch went up by over 70 per cent in high-action areas, compared to under seven per cent in no-action areas, and five per cent in the comparison cities. Could the increased Neighbourhood Watch membership in the high action areas actually have contributed to the Safer Cities effect?

Table 5.1 Survey – change in membership of Neighbourhood Watch schemes, by burglary action intensity

	Safer Cities Burglary action intensity score					Comparison Cities
	none	low	medium	high	all	none
	<£1	£1–13	£13–£70			
Percentage households burgled one or more times in past year						
Before (1990)	17.0	24.1	17.1	17.2	18.8	18.3
After (1992)	18.2	24.8	13.7	29.6	20.8	19.3
Percentage change (before to after)	+7	+3	-20	+72	+11	+5
No. of EDs	163	58	36	23	280	126
No. Schemes	0	34	40	41	96	0
Weighted Data Unweighted N	3,138	1,134	590	710	5,576	2,099

Source: 1990 and 1992 Safer Cities Surveys, SCP Management Information System, 1991 Census.

See Table 2.1 for general explanatory notes.

We did not have direct information on the number of Watch schemes in operation in our survey locations. But we were able to investigate further by making some reasonable assumptions. We judged that EDs in which no respondent, either before or after, said that they belonged to a Watch scheme, in fact *never* had a Watch scheme present. For the remaining areas, those in which only those respondents in the *After*-survey said they were members, we considered to have '*new*' Watch schemes. EDs where respondents in the Before-survey said they were members were regarded as '*old*' schemes, and these were assumed to have kept going a further two years through to the After-survey, even if no after respondents admitted membership.

Out of the 406 surveyed EDs, *96* never had Neighbourhood Watch, *246* had 'old' schemes and *64* had 'new' schemes. The proportion of EDs in the high burglary action set, which had new Watch schemes, was no different from the proportion in the other ED sets. This indicated that the increase in membership in the high action areas shown in Table 5.1 was more likely due to a growth in membership in existing schemes, than to a growth in the number of Watch schemes themselves.

We explored the possible contribution of Neighbourhood Watch to the Safer Cities effect on burglary, by modifying our main statistical model (from the survey). Action was represented simply as low, medium or high, and we compared the after-effects of each of these bands of action, under three conditions: *old* Neighbourhood Watch, *new* Neighbourhood Watch and *never* Neighbourhood Watch.

Among *high*-action areas, we found *no difference* in the reduction in burglary risk, between those with old Neighbourhood Watch schemes, new Watch schemes and those without any at all. However, *low and middle* action areas only showed a reduction in risk when Neighbourhood Watch was present (whether old or new). Neighbourhood Watch may therefore have been a necessary ingredient for lesser amounts of Safer Cities burglary action to work, while more intense action seemed to function adequately alone.

This may help explain the impact of the mere presence of Safer Cities action (Neighbourhood Watch may have shored it up in places), and is consistent with the better performance of 'target-hardening-plus-other' *burglary* action, and 'burglary action-plus' action against *other* crime problems. (Alternatively, the presence of Neighbourhood Watch may have made no contribution in itself, but merely indicated greater social cohesion in an area capable of founding a Watch scheme. The *cohesion* may have been the necessary ingredient.)

The *overall* effect of Neighbourhood Watch (with or without Safer Cities burglary schemes present in the area) seemed to be associated with an *increase* in risk. But it did appear that the presence of tangible Safer Cities burglary action was necessary for Neighbourhood Watch to work.[1] (However, we did *not* set out to conduct a full and fair test on the effectiveness of Neighbourhood Watch, it must be said.)

Comparison with the Kirkholt burglary prevention project is instructive here (Forrester et al., 1988, 1990). This demonstrated that a combination of Neighbourhood Watch and target-hardening worked well.

Domestic security

People were also asked, in the After-survey only, about a range of crime prevention measures they had taken in their home over the previous two years, or which their landlords had taken for them.[2] We focussed on the kinds of measures implemented within the Safer Cities schemes in the surveyed areas – mostly door locks, bolts, chains and viewers, and window

---

1   This could have been a product of the earlier assumption that *old* Watch schemes were all still running – some might have been dead, and unfairly dragging the estimated impact of Watch schemes down. Splitting the old schemes into high-growth schemes and those whose growth in membership was less than 10 percentage points (including those showing negative growth), revealed no drastic difference, although the high-growth Watch scheme areas with low or medium amounts of Safer Cities burglary action did show a greater reduction in risk than their low-growth counterparts.

2   A similar, but less precise, question was asked in both Before and After-surveys. There was a marked increase in security measures in high action EDs, but an increase of the same order in the comparison cities. Low action EDs puzzlingly showed a decrease.

locks. In some cases, the Safer Cities scheme had been directly involved in supplying and fitting the equipment; in others, there was more 'promotional' activity in publicising available devices.

From the survey data, we calculated a score representing the number of such measures installed. Table 5.2 shows that the average number of measures installed is greater in the high action areas. The relatively large number of measures in the Safer Cities areas without action is puzzling, but might be explained by households' own response to the marked growth in crime there. It could also reflect the influence of the burglary prevention campaigns and other action implemented by Safer Cities co-ordinators at the city-wide level. But this is difficult to prove.

Table 5.2 Survey – selected domestic crime prevention measures installed in last two years (after survey only), by burglary action intensity

	Safer Cities Burglary action intensity score					Comparison Cities
	none	low <£1	medium £1–£13	high £13–£70	all	none
Average no. measures† installed per household in past 2 years						
After only	**0.79**	**0.69**	**0.86**	**0.95**	**0.79**	**0.72**
No. of EDs	163	58	36	23	280	126
No. Schemes	0	34	40	41	96	0
Weighted Data Unweighted N	3,138	1,134	590	710	5,576	2,099

Source: 1990 and 1992 Safer Cities Surveys, SCP Management Information System, 1991 Census.

See Table 2.1 for general explanatory notes.
†Measures specifically supplied, fitted or promoted in the action areas: outside doors strengthened or with strengthened frames, with double locks or deadlocks, security chains or bolts, peep hole viewers; windows with security locks; security marking of valuable possessions.

Perceptions of local area

Safer Cities was also intended to improve general community life. Although burglary is only one kind of crime – and 'incivilities' such as litter and vandalism have been shown to be more closely associated with people's feelings about their area – the results are interesting. People were asked to say whether the area within 10 minutes' walk of their home was a good or a bad place to live (Table 5.3). There were increases in the proportion perceiving their locality as bad in every type of area surveyed, including the comparison cities, *except* the areas receiving high levels of burglary action, which showed a 13 per cent decrease. There appears to be a threshold below which action fails to make people feel happier about their surroundings. Indeed, below that threshold, it may serve only to draw attention to an area's problems.

Table 5.3 Survey – assessment of local neighbourhood, by burglary action intensity

	Safer Cities					Comparison
	Burglary action intensity score					Cities
	none	low	medium	high	all	none
		<£1	£1–£13	£13–£70		
Percentage believe they live in bad area[+]						
Before (1990)	27.4	20.6	23.1	28.3	25.4	27.4
After (1992)	28.3	25.6	35.3	24.7	28.0	30.5
% change						
(before to after)	+3	+24	+53	-13	+10	+11
No. of EDs	163	58	36	23	280	126
No. Schemes	0	34	40	41	96	0
Weighted Data						
Unweighted N	3,138	1,134	590	710	5,576	2,099

Source: 1990 and 1992 Safer Cities Surveys, SCP Management Information System, 1991 Census.

See Table 2.1 for general explanatory notes.
+   Respondents were asked to rate whether or not area within 10 minutes walking distance from home was a 'bad place to live'

Worry about burglary

Reducing fear of crime was the second Safer Cities objective. So what about the effect of Safer Cities on worry about burglary? In brief, the results indicate little overall benefit in reducing worry. However, among those – and they were the minority – who were aware of some action being taken, worry was reduced where the action was of a higher intensity.

Table 5.4 shows, first, the lack of any overall effect of action on worry as measured by the surveys. Indeed, worry about burglary fell more in the comparison cities. Those in areas selected for action were significantly more worried about burglary initially, and this is not surprising. But the more action was taken the significantly *more* worried householders were in the After-surveys. For instance 69 per cent of householders in high-action EDs said they were worried in the Before-survey, as against 74 per cent in the

After-survey. Why did this occur? One possibility is that co-ordinators had targetted areas where fear was rising. Another is that action itself awakened fear by focussing attention on the burglary problem.

Table 5.4 Survey – worry about burglary among whole sample and by those actually aware of existence of crime prevention schemes, by burglary action intensity

	Safer Cities Burglary action intensity score					Comparison Cities
	none	low	medium	high	all	none
		<£1	£1–£13	£13–£70		
Percentage worried or very worried about burglary in area						
Before (1990)	67.5	71.4	72.5	69.4	69.2	71.2
After (1992)	69.3	69.1	73.7	74.1	70.3	68.6
percentage change (before to after)	+3	-3	+2	+7	+2	-4
percentage change (those aware of some action+)	0	+10	-6	-9	+1	-17
No. of EDs	163	58	36	23	280	126
No. Schemes	0	34	40	41	96	0
Weighted Data Unweighted N	3,138	1,134	590	710	5,576	2,099
N (aware)	633	259	107	212	1,211	424

Source: 1990 and 1992 Safer Cities Surveys, SCP Management Information System, 1991 Census.

See table 2.1 for general explanatory notes.

[+] 'Aware of any crime prevention schemes in locally or city'. This may or may not be Safer cities action.

There is an important difference, though, between those people in scheme areas who were aware of action, and those who were not. As Table 5.5 shows, awareness of action is uniformly low – and this is of any kind of preventive action, implemented by any agency, anywhere in the city or borough. (We had to use this general measure since very few in the After-survey said they knew of 'Safer Cities' schemes specifically. Using the general measure meant that people could report being aware of 'any' action at the time of the Before-survey.) Moreover, in almost all conditions there is a before-to-after *fall* in the proportion of respondents who report being aware of any action in their city or borough. In the After-survey, 14 per cent of respondents in the comparison cities reported being aware of some preventive action in their local area, or city; this was very similar to those in Safer Cities as a whole (15%). Only in Safer Cities EDs which received *high* action, was there an *increase* in awareness (from 17% to 25%).

Table 5.5 Survey – awareness of schemes introduced in city/
borough over past two years, by burglary action intensity

	Safer Cities Burglary action intensity score					Comparison Cities
	none	low	medium	high	all	none
		<£1	£1–£13	£13–£70		
Percentage aware						
Before (1990)	20.7	24.0	18.2	16.6	20.7	20.7
After (1992)	13.7	14.6	14.4	25.1	15.4	14.0
Percentage change	**-34**	**-33**	**-21**	**+51**	**-26**	**-32**
No. of EDs	163	58	36	23	280	126
No. Schemes	0	34	40	41	96	0
Weighted Data Unweighted N	3,138	1,134	590	710	5,576	2,099

Source: 1990 and 1992 Safer Cities Surveys, SCP Management Information System, 1991 Census.

See Table 2.1 for general explanatory notes.

We looked at whether there was a 'Safer Cities effect' on worry separately for those who were and were not aware of preventive action, as broadly defined. This showed (Table 5.4) that generally people who were aware of any action experienced reduced worry. Further, the more Safer Cities action was taken, the less they were worried. The one exception to this was the people in the low-action EDs: they showed a nearly 10 per cent rise in worry, even if they were aware of action. It is not easy to explain this.

This picture is broadly confirmed by more detailed statistical analysis which sought to explain variation in people's tendency to report that they were worried or very worried. The statistical model developed was rather similar to that used to analyse the survey prevalence risks, although some additional extraneous factors were taken account of (such as respondents' gender, and whether they lived alone, or had been burgled).

The results of the analysis were rather complicated:

1) People who were aware of preventive action (of *any* kind, anywhere in the locality or the city) had a greater tendency to worry; but their worry was rather less in the After-survey.[3]

2) Safer Cities burglary action tended to be *located* in EDs where people reported high worry.

---

3   This took account of any panel membership. Whilst panel members might be expected to show less worry, since they stayed on in their areas, in fact our panel members showed a greater tendency to worry overall, and an increase in the After-survey.

3) There was a somewhat *reduced* tendency to be worried following action, but this applied only to the *presence* of action. The *amount* of action was associated with the *opposite* effect: areas receiving more intense action showed an *increase* in worry (relative to those receiving less intense action).[4]

4) The pattern in 2) and 3) *reversed* for people who were aware of (any) action. For them, worry *increased* after action was present (step effect). But people in areas receiving *more intense action* tended, after implementation, to show *decreased* worry.

What can be made of these findings, and those from Table 5.4? There are difficulties in establishing a firm link between people's general awareness of crime prevention action, and their awareness of Safer Cities action in particular. Nevertheless, it is helpful to try to establish a coherent view, even if it has to be a fairly speculative one.

- First, it seems that unless action is particularly intensive, or of a public nature such as Neighbourhood Watch, people remain unaware of what is being done, even if it is in their immediate locality (a similar lack of awareness was reported in the Scottish Safer Cities Programme (Carnie, 1995)), The only increase in awareness (just over 50%) was in the EDs receiving high action. This seems to have limited the impact of Safer Cities schemes generally on worry about burglary.

- Second, where people are aware of action, that action will only have a measurably beneficial effect on worry if it is substantial either in terms of the numbers of households targetted, or the amount of action per household, or both. This action may serve to reduce worry either indirectly, by reducing 'real' burglary risk, or directly (and subjectively), by convincing people that something substantial is being done to tackle their local burglary problem. Weak action (or action implemented in only a few households in the neighbourhood) may serve only to draw attention to burglary without reassuring those few householders who are aware of it, that something is being done for them. This may be so even though (as our earlier analysis showed) it is the presence of action as much as the amount which reduces *objective* burglary risk. From the statistical model, our best estimate of the threshold intensity above which people aware of prevention show reduced worry, was about £20 per household.

---

4   This pattern was true for burglary action alone in an area, burglary plus other Safer Cities action, and other Safer Cities action alone. This suggested that the type of action did not greatly matter in influencing people's worry

6 The question of mechanism: what produced the Safer Cities effect on burglary?

Among the findings we have so far reported are the following:

- Both main analyses of Safer Cities' impact on burglary – survey and recorded crime – suggested that the presence of action was as important in reducing risk as the intensity of action, if not more so.

- There was only limited awareness of the Safer Cities Programme and local preventive action among those exposed to it.

- There was only a modest tendency for households within the Safer Cities action areas to report having more home security measures installed during the main phase of Safer Cities activity.

- 'Mixed' action against burglary seemed to perform better than target-hardening alone (although target-hardening did work independently).

- Other Safer Cities action (not targetted on burglary) seemed to have an important role in shoring up the effects of the burglary action on burglary.

- There was an increase in Neighbourhood Watch membership in high-action areas in the survey, although it was only low levels of action that seemed to need the extra presence of Neighbourhood Watch for the action to reduce risk. And Neighbourhood Watch itself appeared to work only in the presence of tangible Safer Cities action.

- Partial geographic displacement of burglary, by burglary action, seemed to have occurred from action areas to adjacent zones; but also, possibly, there was diffusion of benefit spreading from the action when it was of high intensity. Burglary action in an area seemed to protect against 'inward' geographic displacement of burglary from other burglary schemes in *adjacent* areas, deflecting it elsewhere perhaps; and against crime switch *into* burglary from schemes in the *same* area but targetted on different offences. Low levels of burglary action seemed to cause offenders to switch to other property crimes, but medium-to-high levels of burglary action seemed to reduce these other offences too.

Given all this, how did the Safer Cities schemes have their impact on burglary?

This evaluation was not designed to explore the *causal mechanisms* by which action may have led to outcome (Pawson and Tilley, 1994; Ekblom and Pease, 1995). To that end, a detailed study of individual schemes would have been more suitable. But it is important to try to reconcile the apparent paradox in particular between evidence of impact of Safer Cities action, and evidence of residents' lack of awareness of it. A number of possibilities emerge, relating to measurement issues as much as to mechanisms themselves.

Measurement issues

- Experience of surveys suggests people are often surprisingly unaware of action taken in and around their own homes. Respondents may say, simply, that 'the Council did something...'; or some other member of their family may have been present when the installation occurred. Quite a number of the target-hardening schemes involved the elderly, and this may have further reduced awareness of action, for example where retirement homes, with communal security fittings such as lighting, were concerned.

- Some of the kinds of security measures installed by Safer Cities – fences, communal entryphones etc. – were not covered by the survey question results reported in Table 5.3.[1]

- In many schemes, areas were not subjected to 'blanket coverage' – only the homes of those at risk (e.g. existing burglary victims) or those judged to be vulnerable (e.g. the elderly) were targetted (Sutton, 1996). This 'sprinkling' of action would not necessarily be noticed by members of the households it passed by. However, it could still affect the risk experienced by those households, as described below.

---

1. Fence installation or repair – a question asked of council tenants only – did show a marked increase in the high-action areas.

Mechanisms

- Preventive action against burglary may operate at two levels – *individual* and *area* – and in two ways – heightening *objective* effort and risk to burglars, and heightening *subjective* perceptions of effort and risk. With the protection of *individual* homes, the Safer Cities action could have physically blocked the offence, or made the offence seem more risky and less rewarding to the burglar. At the *area* level, offenders may perceive that security has been enhanced in a particular neighbourhood, and avoid the whole area (Rhodes and Conly, 1981). Whether the area is objectively more risky for them (bristling with active neighbourhood watchers scanning across improved sight-lines, perhaps), or whether the risk is only a subjective one (the mere knowledge that something has been done to tackle burglary in an area) may not matter (cf Laycock 1985 and 1992) on the mechanisms behind an apparent impact of property). Individual householders need not be aware of the presence of action in their neighbourhood, nor even of security measures installed in their homes for the action to have its impact through subjective enhancement of risks to offenders.

- If householders seem not to be aware of preventive action, how is it that burglars are? Burglars may simply be more sensitive to changes in security measures than honest residents. One recent study has, in fact, demonstrated that burglars were markedly better than non-burglars at recognising security changes, such as fitting of new locks, to photographed houses (Wright et al., 1995).

- Many of the findings from both survey and recorded crime seem to point to the operation of area processes. Displacement to adjacent areas, diffusion of benefit, 'protective' effects of existing burglary action in an area (against both displacement and crime switch into burglary) all suggest this. Diffusion of benefit in particular implies that offenders are being guided by illusory risks beyond the boundaries of objective action, when that action is of sufficiently high intensity. The lack of any increase in concentration (repeat victimisation), as measured by the survey, again suggests that if there is any displacement, it is on an area-to-area basis not from hardened households to more vulnerable ones nearby. The better performance of mixed methods rather than 'pure' target–hardening, and the importance of support from 'other' Safer Cities action suggest that specific security improvements on specific homes may not always be enough to achieve reductions in risk (a finding consistent with the experience of the Kirkholt project (Forrester et al., 1988, 1990)).

- The scale of the effect of the *mere presence* of Safer Cities action is also consistent with an area process, although the marginal-intensity effect of extra action could be either area or individual. It is, however, possible that much of the 'step' effect – the reduction in risk due to the presence of action – owes its existence to a kind of 'shoring up' of the impact of low intensity anti-burglary action by other influences in the area. These include the presence of Safer Cities action against other crime problems, and Neighbourhood Watch.

Having presented all this evidence suggestive of the importance of area processes, it should be said, though, that our approach to measuring action intensity at the area level *predisposes* us to focus on areas. It should therefore be borne in mind that our findings are not proof *against* the operation of processes at household-level, such as the physical defence of an individual home enhanced by target-hardening, and the heightened risk of discovery the offender perceives at that site. Preventive strategies that are known to act on an individual household basis – such as the target-hardening of known repeat-victimised households (Farrell and Pease, 1994) – should not neglect the possibility of exploiting the area dimension, and vice versa. Indeed, given the finding that areas with high crime rates tend to have a greater concentration of incidents on repeat victims (Trickett et al., 1992), the two targetting processes naturally go together.

7 Points of discussion

A comprehensive summary of findings and conclusions is at the beginning of this report. This last part develops the discussion of a number of aspects of the evaluation and the results.

The fairly 'typical' Safer Cities burglary prevention schemes evaluated here seemed to reduce the risk of burglary. The mere presence of action was as significant as the intensity of action – perhaps more so. The *overall* cost per burglary prevented – albeit estimated with a fairly wide latitude of uncertainty – was under most conditions rather less than the direct financial costs of that burglary to the household and the CJS. In areas with higher risk rates, the *marginal* cost, of preventing one more burglary by investing more funds at the inception of a scheme, was also close to, or less than the cost of the burglary itself.[1] Overall, the *cost* of preventing a burglary diminished in areas where burglary was more common, although reducing the *risk* of burglary seemed in some cases to become more difficult.

Cost-effectiveness – qualifications and assumptions

This positive picture is based on an analysis of large and complex sets of data. Inevitably, we have had to make judgements about the weight to attach to various uncertainties and biases in the analysis, the plausibility of alternative explanations for the findings, and the assumptions about costing in particular. This is not the place to rehearse the uncertainties, which do give wide margins of error, and which could not have been significantly reduced without inordinate cost and more than a little benefit of hindsight. But it is worth recalling the key costing assumptions we had to make, to help future decision-makers come to their own conclusions and as an aid to generalising our findings to other community safety contexts.

Our cost estimates include Safer Cities running costs, and the costs of implementing city-wide schemes such as publicity campaigns. The running

---

1   This does not imply that investing more money in new schemes in the same area, or even re-invigorating an existing scheme at a later date, would have the same effect at the margin. Money spent in this way may be more cost-effective than the same money had it been spent on enlarging the original scheme at its inception. However, such possibilities go beyond our analysis.

costs were obviously necessary in bringing the evaluated schemes about. The city-wide action could also have helped to establish the right 'partnership' climate of interest and co-operation for the schemes to work best. The costs also include levered funds, for example from other local and national programmes, that the Safer Cities co-ordinators succeeded in obtaining. Any contribution from individual householders, such as their *own* expenditure on security equipment, would have been a further cost input (albeit not from Government); but it was not possible to distinguish self-financed purchases from installation funded by Safer Cities or any other agency. The increased participation in Neighbourhood Watch in high-action surveyed areas seemed not to have contributed to the Safer Cities effect in those locations, but may have done so in the low and medium action areas.

Five other points about the cost estimates are worth noting.

First, there was a tendency for many of the schemes we looked at to be *clustered,* due to co-ordinators' strategic implementation policies, a tendency amplified by our selection of some of the surveyed EDs on the basis of co-ordinators' guidance; this clustering may have improved their effectiveness, as the analysis (of burglary-plus other action) suggested.[2] Schemes implemented in isolation may be somewhat less effective (although analysis was unable to confirm this). Certainly, our estimates depend heavily on the presence of other Safer Cities action. However, such clustering and overlapping of action can be used to advantage (as discussed under displacement, below).

Second, one of the most important uncertainties which remains concerns the *durability* of preventive action. We made a conservative assumption of two years, but longer duration would increase cost-effectiveness of action in direct proportion. There was some suggestion from the recorded crime analysis that action of lesser intensity had less durable effects, but this would need to be explored further (through a fresh data-collection exercise). Whatever the case, our consideration of mechanisms did indicate that 'illusory' perception of risk may have been responsible for deterring offenders from some Safer Cities action areas. Such security illusions may well be short-term.

Third is the possibility that co-ordinators targetted areas where there was *greater community willingness to fight crime* (Sutton, 1996). On the larger scale, the Home Office itself deliberately selected cities for membership of the Programme which had a history of involvement in prevention. Either

---

2   The areas selected by *co-ordinators* for inclusion in the survey on the basis of being planned foci of action (in contrast to the survey areas chosen from high-crime ACORN subcategories) showed, in the statistical model, an additional reduction in burglary risk independent of our measures of the Safer Cities effect. Our estimates of cost-effectiveness may understate the total benefit from Safer Cities action, since they take no account of this extra gain.

factor may have given a hidden boost to the Safer Cities effect.

Fourth, some uncertainty remains about *displacement* of various kinds. Preventive action of the kind implemented through Safer Cities will always have to be targeted on particular crimes in particular areas, for economic reasons. 'Wall-to-wall' coverage of the entire city, which might limit any geographical displacement of crime, is out of the question in practical terms. We found some limited evidence of geographical displacement from the areas covered by Safer Cities burglary schemes, which would, if taken into account, reduce our estimates of cost-effectiveness. But this was by no means the pessimistic picture of universal and inevitable displacement painted by some critics of prevention, which would neutralise all localised benefits of reduced crime. In particular, where action was intensive, there seemed to be mitigation of between-area displacement due to 'diffusion of benefit' – the desired impact of preventive action extending *beyond* its intended boundaries. In the meantime, even if some crimes were displaced to other areas, there are good grounds for trying to deflect them from the worst-affected households or localities, as Safer Cities has been seeking to do. Deflection can be turned to further advantage if used strategically. We found some evidence of a process we called *'security enveloping',* in which adjacent action from different schemes seemed to create a wider protected area avoided by offenders, with preventive effects greater than the sum of individual contributions.

'Outward' *crime switch* (frustrated burglars changing to other crimes) seemed to occur where burglary action was only of low intensity. There was some evidence of 'inward' crime switch (action targetted on other crimes causing offenders to take up burglary) in areas themselves unprotected by burglary action.

The fifth issue is our assumption that neither crime prevention activity *outside the Safer Cities Programme,* nor wider urban action, *systematically* influenced where Safer Cities burglary action was located (and vice versa). Had Safer Cities action been consistently directed towards areas with other action, for example, this could have unfairly boosted the estimate of impact and reduced the apparent cost of prevention. A full-scale attempt to collect data on other action proved beyond our resources (in fact, the Safer Cities Management Information System appeared, despite its faults and doubts about the consistency of some of the entries, to be a far better local database than that possessed by other large-scale initiatives such as the Urban Programme). But it was argued on the basis of interviews with co-ordinators that there was no systematic tendency across the Programme for Safer Cities action to be directed towards, or away from other interventions.

Less tangible benefits?

Less tangible gains in high-action areas, in any event, may include reduced worry, and increased confidence which may be reflected in wider social and economic benefits in the area. It needs to be said, here, that the findings on worry were not straightforward. It is quite usual for crime prevention evaluations to report little impact on crime but, as a 'consolation prize', that worry or fear went down. Paradoxically, this study found the reverse – tangible effects on crime, but little consistent impact on worry or on perceptions of improvement in the neighbourhood. The key to this seemed to be the overall lack of awareness of action except where this was most intensive. Future interventions should make sure that householders are aware that action is being taken. Such a message might have an additional effect in deterring offenders. (Tilley and Webb (1994) also emphasised the importance of publicity in these respects.) It goes without saying, though, that the protection delivered needs to be credible to both householders and to burglars. Among the minority of householders that were aware of action, low levels of action seemed actually to raise worry.

Political constraints may also be important here. Co-ordinators and their steering committees were often concerned with issues of inequity ('why should one house, or one area, get preventive action, and not another?') (Sutton, 1996). Publicity could exacerbate this. Under such circumstances, it is important to establish a clear and defensible policy, in consultation with those residents with a stake in security. (One example is the policy of targetting on repeat victims – they are seen as most deserving, as they have already suffered and are particularly likely to suffer burglary again (cf. Farrell and Pease, 1994).) Since benefits to the whole area may emerge from action on individual homes or streets (as the limited evidence for diffusion of benefit, and the 'step' effect of Safer Cities action both suggest), this message could be stressed. However, monitoring against the possibility of home-to-home displacement should also be offered as part of the package.

Is the mere presence of burglary action really enough?

Finally, it is worth briefly returning to consider the separate effects on risk of the presence and the intensity of action. It may be, as already stated, that the step is not so much a quantum drop as a very steep downward slope in risk as action intensity increases from, say, a penny per household to a pound. But this is difficult to measure against background variation between areas; and, as already mentioned, even a penny-worth of intensity produced a clear drop in risk. Certainly mechanisms to explain the impact of the Safer Cities burglary schemes, which focus on offenders' perceptions of action in an area, are compatible with either a step or a steep slope.

As regards the implications of a step, if the mere presence of action were enough to bring about a sizeable reduction in burglary, then why invest any more than the bare minimum in an area? Perhaps simply putting preventive posters through letter-boxes might suffice to bring about the step reduction in risk? There are two considerations why this is not the case.

First, there is evidence from several directions that the step effect of burglary action may have been supported, with action of low and medium intensity, by the presence of Safer Cities action against other crime problems, and by Neighbourhood Watch (or alternatively, the favourable social conditions that often go with the presence of Watch schemes). Second, whatever the case, having more than the minimum of burglary action seems worthwhile, to exploit diffusion of benefit, to prevent crime switch from burglary to other property crimes, and to reassure those concerned about burglary that what was being done was enough to be credible. All these beneficial processes seemed to depend on higher-intensity action.

Other evaluation issues

The evaluation broke new ground in linking 'micro' analysis of small areas, and the action they received, to the 'macro' scale of cities and to the overall performance of a major programme of prevention. Two very different sources of outcome measures – surveys and recorded crime statistics – produced answers which were in most cases remarkably similar, although some loose ends in the evaluation inevitably remain. Finally, burglary was, as explained at the beginning, the 'best bet'. We have yet to see whether action targetted on other kinds of crime has the same measurable impact.

This said, Phase 1 of the Safer Cities Programme seems to have achieved an impact on burglary through interventions by local agencies with relatively limited experience of practical crime prevention, in the absence of particularly efficient targetting, and without full exploitation of deterrence through offenders' awareness of action. Given this, the potential for further gains in Phase 2 of the Safer Cities Programme is considerable. In a context where in the past few large-scale interventions against social problems seem to have much measurable effect, this is good news.

End notes

1. Generating action intensity scores: scoping and scoring

A central premise in this evaluation was that the local Safer Cities burglary schemes had to be 'capable' of affecting the outcome measures. Using information from the Safer Cities Management Information System (MIS), schemes had to meet the following criteria:

- they had to target the relevant crime problem - i.e. domestic burglary

- they had to be 'current' or 'completed': cancelled or aborted schemes, and those judged by co-ordinators to have been inadequately implemented, were weeded out

- they had to involve action on the ground, not conferences or research alone

- they had to have started prior to the 'After' survey, or in a given year for which we had collected beat-level recorded crime data ('started' was carefully defined in the MIS manual as the time at which the action began exerting itself on the ground–distinguished, for example, from the (earlier) time the implementation team was set up)

- they had to be judged by co-ordinators as having the potential to reduce crime in the short-to-medium term, not merely after several years as with some 'developmental' action

- they had to cover a territory which overlapped with one or more of the surveyed areas, or (with the analysis of recorded crime data) one of the police beats.

The units in which these overlaps in time and space were identified, were the *month* and the *1991 Census Enumeration District* (some 200 households). The territory of a scheme, known as its *'Zone of Influence'*, was identified by the co-ordinators on large-scale maps. The surveyed Enumeration Districts, and the police beat-years for which recorded crime data was collected, were known as *'Zones of Detection'*. Further details are in Ekblom and Pease (1995: Appendix).

Figure N1.1 1991 Enumeration District map of Coventry

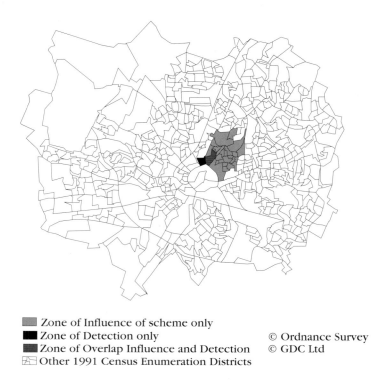

◾ Zone of Influence of scheme only
◾ Zone of Detection only   © Ordnance Survey
▦ Zone of Overlap Influence and Detection   © GDC Ltd
⬡ Other 1991 Census Enumeration Districts

Each scheme which met these criteria was known as being 'in scope'. An action intensity score was generated for the scheme, in each of the Zones of Detection with which it overlapped. (The overlapping area was called the *'Zone of Overlap'*; Figure N1.1 shows the relationship between Zones of Influence, Detection and Overlap.) The score took account of the total funds spent (known from the Safer Cities MIS) and the respective numbers of households in the Zones of Influence and Detection (taken from Census Small-Area Statistics linked to information on scheme location from co-ordinators, purchased ED boundary data and beat maps digitised by ourselves). Schemes were assumed to exert an influence for at least two years after starting. Scores were adjusted down if schemes started part-way through the 12–month 'recall period' covered by the 'After' survey, or the relevant 12–month crime-recording period. This gave the *average intensity of action input to which households in the area were exposed over a whole year.* Where an area was the focus of more than one scheme, the individual contributions were added.

For example, take a scheme whose total cost of £10,000 was shared out over a Zone of Influence of five 1991 EDs together comprising 1,000 households. Each household would receive on average an action input of £10. Suppose 200 of these households were in an ED that overlapped with a beat Zone of Detection of 800 households. Given that we did not know which of these 800 households had received the action (we could not disaggregate the crime data below beat level), we again took an average: each of these households was assumed to receive 200/800 worth of the action input – ie a dilution factor of four. If the action did not begin until halfway through the crime recording year, it was diluted by a further factor of two. All this gave the average input of scheme funds per household in the beat, over the relevant year of measurement (i.e., the beat-year), of £1.25. As a formula:

$$\frac{\text{Scheme cost (£) x households in Zone of Overlap x months of overlap}}{\text{households in Zone of Influence x households in Zone of Detection x 12 months crime recording year}}$$

The action score from a single widespread scheme could cover two or more beats in a given city. However, these beats need not have the same score. For example, the Zone of Influence of the scheme could overlap fully with the Zone of Detection of one beat, but only cover half the territory of another. (This is because our territories of action location – 1991 EDs – were considerably smaller than beats.) The intensity of action 'seen', on average, by the second beat will only be half that seen by the first. Therefore, while the action is assumed to be constant over the scheme's Zone of Influence, its average measured levels may differ across the Zones of Detection it covers. Similar considerations applied to the surveyed EDs, because the 1981 EDs which comprised our survey Zones of Detection sometimes covered the territory of two or three 1991 EDs (see end note 4).

This 'scoping and scoring' exercise was conducted by purpose-built software on an Arc/Info geographic information system and relational database (Ekblom, 1994; Ekblom and Pease, 1995; Ekblom, Howes and Law, 1994; Howes, 1994). A range of alternative assumptions can be programmed into the scoping and scoring (for example, incorporating a delay before schemes 'bite'), and further exploration of these parameters may enable better 'tuning' to detect the strongest Safer Cities 'signal' and improve upon the accuracy of current estimates of the Safer Cities effect.

2. The survey data

The 7,679 interviews in the survey were supplied by 5,835 adult residents from households identified through the Postal Address File (MORI 1990, 1993). The panel – 1,844 respondents – gave interviews both before and after. The overall response rate was 60 per cent, despite strenuous efforts to increase this proportion, reflecting the high-crime areas surveyed. Of the 280 Safer Cities EDs selected for survey, 103 were identified by the co-ordinators (they identified 16 neighbourhoods in nine Safer Cities; surveys in each neighbourhood were clustered in groups of up to nine EDs). A third of these EDs overlapped with some action. The remaining 177 EDs (which were not deliberately clustered) were selected from ACORN neighbourhood subcategories which have been shown to be high-risk by the British Crime Survey; almost half of these overlapped with some action. All 126 EDs in the comparison cities were similarly selected on the basis of ACORN/British Crime Survey data.

3. Selection of the Safer Cities and comparison cities and borough for the survey

Selection of the Safer Cities for the survey was basically a matter of timing. We needed to choose those cities which had recently started up (to minimise the amount of action in place prior to our Before-survey). On the other hand, we did not want cities whose co-ordinator was either not in place yet, or who had little idea where action was planned. The Safer Cities finally surveyed were Birmingham, Bristol, Coventry, Hull, Rochdale, Salford, Sunderland; and the London Boroughs of Lewisham, Tower Hamlets and Wandsworth.

Selection of the comparison cities and boroughs (Hackney, Southwark, Haringey, Manchester, North Tyneside, Wigan, Oldham and Leeds) was a multi-stage process. Like the Safer Cities, the comparison cities were drawn from the 57 'Urban Priority areas'. These are local authority districts which showed significant deprivation based on indicators from the 1981 Census. Candidate comparison cities were eliminated if they had been selected for other recent major preventive action – in particular Crime Concern's area crime reduction projects. Then, the remainder were stratified on the basis of Craig's (1985) families of local authority districts (derived from a cluster analysis of 1981 Census data), and those in the same family groups as the surveyed Safer Cities cities (plus a 'London' group) were retained for the next stage. Here, per capita recorded crime rates over the previous five years (from data collected by Home Office Statistics divisions) were used to try to put together a set (within each Census family) of comparison cities whose crime rates were consistently similar to those of the corresponding Safer Cities cities. Finally, there was a need to avoid selecting comparison cities which might be chosen as the final four Safer Cities. (Although timing was critical on this, only one of the originally-selected comparison cities –

Middlesbrough – was lost by subsequently entering the Safer Cities Programme.) The number of cities available by this stage had become limited, but the match achieved was felt to be reasonable (Ekblom (1991, 1992) gives further details.)

4. Getting 1981 ED action scores for the survey: Linking 1981 EDs to 1991 EDs

Since the sampling had to be done in 1990, the EDs sampled in the surveys were those defined in the 1981 Census. Also, their selection relied on 1981-standard ACORN data (with the exception of those identified by co-ordinators). Unfortunately, a large proportion of EDs had their boundaries changed, fused or split for the 1991 Census (the standard we adopted necessarily for the Census data, and for the scheme location data). Our solution was to:

• identify which *1991* ED each respondent lived in (using their postcode, and the postcode-ED directory)

• calculate action scores on the basis of 1991 EDs

• assign these scores to individual survey respondents on the basis of their 1991 ED

• average these 1991 scores over all the respondents in a single 1981 ED.

This produced a 1981 ED action score, weighted in proportion to the respondents residing in each 'daughter' 1991 ED. The process clearly resulted in some blurring of the measurement of action, but was felt to give a sufficient measure of the action in the 1981 EDs.

5. Weighting of tabular data from the survey (applies to Tables 2.1, 2.2, 5.1–5.5)

The *tabular data* was weighted to reflect sampling considerations. This meant weighting down the relative contribution to any survey estimates of risk, from cities which had greater numbers of sampling points (surveyed EDs). It also meant the combined comparison cities' burglary risks were adjusted to make their Census family composition (see end note 3) match that of the Safer Cities.

6. Linking recorded crime data with the survey to study regression-to-the-mean

Recorded crime data in some years, and/or some beats, were not collected: the approximate proportion of surveyed EDs covered in the Safer Cities ranged from 1/3 in 1987 to 1/2 in 1990. The number of beats contributing to the recorded crime data ranged from 68 in 1987 to 113 in 1990. The only surveyed Safer City which had no matching recorded crime data at all was

Wandsworth. To avoid irrelevant variation, only those beats and EDs were included in the analysis which had the complete four-year series of recorded crime data linked to an ED.

In order to bypass another source of error, the survey-to-beat linkage was done using the *1991* ED boundaries, which were the original basis for calculating the Safer Cities action scores, rather than the 1981 ED boundaries, which were used in the survey analysis as explained elsewhere.

7. Taking account of prior burglary prevalence in the survey model

This is a variation of a technique known as 'regression adjustment' (Judd and Kenny, 1981), or 'conditional regression'. This is normally used when analysing individual-level panel data, where each panel respondent's after-response is the dependent variable, and the before-response is one of the explanatory variables. We adapted it to area-level analysis because i) a sizeable proportion of our respondents were not in the panel (so it would have been wasteful and limiting to focus just on the panel subset), and ii) we were particularly interested in area-level relationships.

For each surveyed ED, we calculated the average burglary prevalence revealed by the interviews in the *Before*-survey. We then included this in the model, to explain the variation in victimisation common to the interviews in the same ED in the *After*-survey. In effect, this was a term in the model equivalent to an 'after x area prior burglary risk' interaction.

8. A floor effect?

Any floor effect would not be simply due to running out of numbers of burglary victims in an ED (e.g. 'only two victims in Before-survey, therefore cannot show a big fall in the After-survey'), because – apart from extreme cases – the before and after prevalence rates are only imperfectly correlated. Low burglary risk in an ED in the Before-survey only means a *tendency* towards low risk in the After-survey. Further, the reductions in risk represented in logistic regression concern *proportions* of victims, not absolute numbers. It was possible, however, that the apparent step growth with prior burglary rate was an artifact caused by sampling error. The average number of interviews in the Before-survey was 10 – quite small for estimating the area prevalence of a relatively rare event such as burglary. To explore this further, the terms in the model representing prior burglary risk, and its interaction with Safer Cities action, were omitted for the 59 out of 406 EDs with less than five interviews in the Before-survey. The result of this was to reduce the step's growth with prior burglary risk considerably – and it was no longer statistically significant. This suggests that sampling error may have played some part. However, the shrinkage of the marginal effect with higher prior burglary risk actually became more marked. Explanations centring on regression-to-the-mean have already been discounted.

9. Selection of comparison cities and boroughs for recorded crime analysis

Selection of the comparison cities and boroughs for the recorded crime analysis (Barnsley, Burnley, Hackney, Haringey, Liverpool, Manchester, Oldham, Leeds and Southwark) was done in a very similar way to the selection for the survey (end note 3). There were a few differences, due to the need this time to match to a wider set of Safer Cities, and to the caprices of data availability.

The *first* indicator was based on the Census family, because there was fairly wide divergence in the burglary trends between different Census family groups. For each beat-year, the indicator value was derived from the comparison cities in the appropriate family. Within each *family,* the contributions from the rates of individual comparison *cities* were weighted by household population. The Safer Cities burglary rates followed their family comparison indicators rather well. The *second* indicator was global, applied to Safer Cities beats irrespective of the city these were sited in. Here, the comparison rates were weighted to correspond to the Census family composition of the Safer Cities as a whole. Since the composition varied on a year by year basis (with some beats, and some Safer Cities, not being measured for the whole six years), the weighting was done separately for each year. This applied to both global and family indicators.

Appendix 1:The statistical model for the survey: explaining variation in risk of burglary victimisation

Multi-level models

Applications in multi-level modelling (or hierarchical linear modelling) have grown dramatically over the last decade. The impetus came from the educational context, in which it was important to consider separately those influences on pupils' performance which operated on the individual (e.g. personality), the class (e.g. teacher's style) and the school (e.g. school ethos, nature of catchment area). These 'contextual' influences are described *as levels*. Statistical theory and examples are in Goldstein (1995), and Bryk and Raudenbush (1992). Jones (1992) gives a less technical description.

In the present context, our interest is in a different set of levels: *interview occasions* (level 1), *respondents* (who may have been interviewed more than once) (level 2) and the small *area* sampling points (1981 EDs, level 3) where groups of interviewed respondents lived. The second and third levels are groupings of interviews in a hierarchy. For panel members there will be two observations (interviews) at level 1, but only one for other survey respondents. It is at the area level that we measured the amount of Safer Cities action; we looked for its special effects on the burglary risk observed in the after-interviews, again grouped by area.

In ordinary least squares regression the residual, unexplained variation between *observed* burglary victimisation and victimisation *predicted* by the model would all be represented by a single residual for each case. In multi-level modelling, this variation is split between levels. This takes account of (co-)variation common to groups of cases which would, in an ordinary least squares regression, cause over-estimation of the significance of a term. (The problem, in survey methodology, is known as a 'clustering' effect, and is conventionally taken account of through estimation of the 'design effect'. In practice this provides a correction for the standard error and typically results in conservative significance tests.)

The residual variation between units at any level, and between units, can itself be modelled. By allowing 'regression effects' to vary within units or by implementing a 'random slopes' regression, for any coefficient (such as the coefficient representing the magnitude of the effect of a respondent's age on risk of victimisation), we can assess the extent to which effects are typical across units. For example, we might want to see whether the effect of age on burglary risk *differs* in magnitude across each ED group of interviews. The age term in the model would then be represented in two ways: as a *fixed* component, the 'average' effect of age on the risk of burglary across all interviews, and a *random* component, the 'offset' (or deviation) from this average effect, common only to all those interviews in a given ED. This *variation* results in a variance term, across all EDs, and may be tested to see whether it significantly differs from zero. If it does, we can conclude that the effect of age on burglary risk does indeed vary across ED, and we would then look for ED-level factors which could explain this (e.g. older people live in certain types of area where burglary is more of a problem). If, on the other hand, the age effect did not differ across EDs, we would revert to the simpler model where age had a purely fixed effect. In our models, the only terms we allow to have random values are constants, representing overall 'baseline' burglary risks and their variation between EDs, and between respondents. (We are thus using 'variance components' models.)

Use of three levels enabled us to take full advantage of the embedded panel design. We were able to include data from panelists, and from respondents who appeared only in the Before survey, or only in the After survey. This both maximised numbers of interviews available for analysis, and allowed us to investigate panel processes which seemed to account for an overall reduction in risk from Before to After. Since our data was 'binary response' (i.e. victim/nonvictim) we had to conduct the modelling using logistic regression. This explains the observed variation in the odds of the respondent in a given interview reporting burglary victimisation. (Odds are probability of victimisation / probability of non-victimisation.) We focussed on prevalence risk: techniques for handling the heavily-skewed distribution of incidence counts per respondent are complex and hard to interpret. These basic parameters of the main survey model are shown in Table A1.1.

Table A1.1 Survey model parameters

Dependent variable:	**burglary victim/nonvictim**
Transformation:	**logistic**

Hierarchy	**Units of Analysis**	
Level 3:	**Area (1981 Census ED)**	**N=406**
Level 2:	**Individual Respondent**	**N=5,835**
Level 1:	**Interview Occasion**	**N=7,679**

Embedded panel at level 1– some individuals appear before-only, some after-only, some both

The software package we used for multi-level modelling was ML3E (Prosser et al., 1991), which handles up to three levels. A set of macros to handle 'binary response' was supplied by the package's producers to apply appropriate logistic regression models to our data. ML3E has recently been superseded by MLN, which can handle any number of levels as well as cross-classified designs. It is available from the Institute of Education, University of London.

Explanatory variables: Fixed components

To obtain the best possible estimate of the Safer Cities effect, we left all candidate explanatory variables in the model – we did not simplify the model by dropping those which contributed little to the overall goodness of fit. The fixed components included in the model are listed in Table A1.2. Column 1 of the table lists the relevant variables and interactions included in the model; column 2 the estimates of their coefficients after the model converged; column 3 the standard error of each estimate.

Table A1.2 Fixed components in survey model

VARIABLE IN MODEL	COEFFICIENT ESTIMATE	STANDARD ERROR
LEVEL 1 (INTERVIEW OCCASION) COMPONENT		
After interview	-0.78	0.3595
LEVEL 2 (RESPONDENTS) COMPONENTS		
Constant, all interviews	-3.37	0.5565
L2 Respondent selection		
Member of panel	0.08532	0.1104
After-interview, nonpanelist (L2/L1)	0.3494	0.1554
L2 Respondent demographics		
Over 60-years old	-0.809	0.145
Over 60-years old, after intvw (L2/L1)	0.3999	0.193
High social class	0.3769	0.1623
Managing badly, financially	0.3424	0.1033
Single person household	0.1685	0.08712
Newcomer	0.1734	0.121
[some highly insignificant respondent variables dropped, including gender]		
L2 Respondent area perceptions		
Drugs a problem	0.4515	0.08712
Enough play areas	-0.391	0.1701

Continued...

Table A1.2 Fixed components in survey model (cont.)

VARIABLE IN MODEL	COEFFICIENT ESTIMATE	STANDARD ERROR
LEVEL 3 (ED) COMPONENTS		
L3 1981 ED after-burglary risk explained by average before-risk in same ED (regression adjustment, L3/L1)	2.483	0.5803
L3 Survey area selection by co-ordinators		
Area selected by co-ordinator (SC only)	0.3703	0.1808
...., after-intvw (L3/L1)	-0.1258	0.2518
L3 Area selection by 1981 ED ACORN subcategories		
AC13	0.1652	0.3359
AC16	-0.9217	0.563
AC17	-0.2938	0.5429
AC19	0.06766	0.1984
AC20	-0.05415	0.3654
AC21	-0.4882	0.3233
AC22	-0.09764	0.2305
AC28	-0.2659	0.371
AC29	0.6141	0.3279
AC31	-0.1169	0.3454
AC32	-0.07315	0.4573
ACOTHER	-0.4224	0.3614
L3 ACORN, after-interviews (L3/L1)		
AFAC13	0.02884	0.4811
AFAC16	1.525	0.6817
AFAC17	0.8889	0.731
AFAC19	0.1145	0.2852
AFAC20	0.5634	0.4985
AFAC21	0.6743	0.4226
AFAC22	0.5619	0.3014
AFAC28	0.2846	0.4821
AFAC29	-0.02901	0.4272
AFAC31	1.042	0.4028
AFAC32	0.9554	0.5575
AFACOTHER	1.004	0.4694
L3 1991 ED Census data (converted to 1981 ED boundaries)		
% Black popn	0.00334	0.004197
% Single parent hhold	0.003709	0.004245
% Hhold without car	0.01044	0.008208
% Unemployed popn	0.01295	0.01442
% One person hhold	0.01017	0.007876
% Over 60 popn	-0.02187	0.01077
% Young people 16–24	0.03578	0.01908
Index of Local Conditions (derived from 1991 Census EDs, converted to 1981 ED boundaries)	-0.0691	0.03621

Continued...

Table A1.2 Fixed components in survey model (cont.)

VARIABLE IN MODEL	COEFFICIENT ESTIMATE	STANDARD ERROR
LEVEL 3 CITY FIXED COMPONENTS		
L3 City selection		
Safer City	-1.033	0.3521
Safer City, after-intvw (L3/L1)	0.25	0.2393
Census family 3 (Craig, 1985)		
(London families = baseline)	0.3881	0.4457
Census family 4a	0.9942	0.368
Census family 4b	0.8098	0.3634
Census family 3, after-intvw (L3/L1)	0.03982	0.4548
Census family 4a, after-intvw (L3/L1)	-0.3311	0.2937
Census family 4b, after-intvw (L3/L1)	-0.2794	0.2738
L3 City dummy variables (Hackney = baseline)		
Comparison cities/boroughs:		
Southwark, London	-0.07882	0.2727
Harringey, London	-0.8466	0.33
Manchester	-0.9273	0.42
North Shields	-0.9064	0.4122
Wigan	-1.239	0.4819
Oldham	-0.498	0.3999
Leeds	-1.32	0.4354
Safer Cities (dummies Wandsworth and Wirral excluded due to linear dependency with other variables):		
Birmingham	-0.2066	0.2388
Bristol	0.2234	0.2737
Coventry	-0.4106	0.2269
Hull	-0.4205	0.1888
Lewisham, London	0.3854	0.3172
Salford	0.07459	0.2254
Tower Hamlets, London	0.2627	0.3513

Continued...

Table A1.2 Fixed components in survey model (cont.)

VARIABLE IN MODEL	COEFFICIENT ESTIMATE	STANDARD ERROR
LEVEL 3 SAFER CITIES ACTION COMPONENTS		
L3 other SC action score		
(Safer Cities plus levered funds)		
Other action	-0.004987	0.00465
Other action, after-intvw (L3/L1)	0.005192	0.005931
L3 burglary action score		
(Safer Cities plus levered funds)		
Safer Cities locational effects		
(controlling for assignment of action		
to higher or lower risk areas):		
Step (mere presence of action)	0.2418	0.1781
Marginal (amount of action, given presence)	-0.002966	0.004297
Safer Cities After effects		
(indicating impact as differential reduction		
in risk following action; L3/L1):		
Step (mere presence of action)	*-0.293*	*0.2799*
Special effect of prior burglary risk on step	*-0.8283*	*1.067*
Marginal (amount of action, given presence)	*-0.003*	*0.008794*
Special effect of prior burglary risk on		
marginal	*0.01355*	*0.05407*

A *positive* coefficient estimate for a fixed component indicates that the variable is associated with an *increased* risk of burglary victimisation; a *negative* estimate is associated with a *reduced* risk. The coefficient is the log$_e$ of the multiplier of the odds of victimisation:non-victimisation. Cross-level interactions (mainly x After) are listed under the relevant variables for which they are a subsidiary effect; they are indicated by, for example, L2/L1.

This model has been specially designed for evaluation purposes and is based on a special sample of high-crime areas. Therefore, the observed relationships between the various explanatory variables and burglary risk should not be taken as representative of the country as a whole.

Explanatory variables: Random components

'Before' and 'After', below, are baseline values of burglary risk applying to interviews in the relevant survey wave. Effectively, the terms represent separate intercepts for each wave. Both Before and After terms were included and allowed to vary independently at the ED area level, to enable separate inspection of the variance of the *After* term across EDs. This was particularly important for a model supporting an evaluation design in which some EDs had action and some did not. (Virtually identical results were obtained by fitting a single conventional intercept instead of these two wave terms, although of course it was less easy to see how our explanation of after-variation between EDs was affected by inclusion of particular variables.) After also has a fixed effect (i.e. it appears as a conventional regression coefficient, above); Before does not (Before and After are the two exhaustive values of the same variable, so only one can be included in the fixed part of the model, to avoid redundancy or linear dependence).

The *Level 3* variance of After, for example, is the variation, between EDs, in the coefficient of the intercept for the after-interviews. It represents any distinctive differences, between EDs, in burglary risk measured in the after survey, that are unexplained by the model. As the results below show, this figure is far below its standard error, indicating that there was *no* significant variation in the value of this term between EDs. This is because the large number of fixed area-level terms included in the model (above) accounted for much of the observed variation between EDs. Variation in the After term was much greater in the original 'null model' which contained no Level 3 explanatory variables (see below). By contrast, there remains quite considerable variation between areas in the baseline risk in the Before survey. Apart from anything else, the fact that we are using an ED's average burglary risk in the Before survey to help explain its After risk, means that After will have less unaccounted-for variance than Before. The significant negative covariance between Before and After risk at area level means that EDs which have high risk before tend to be lower risk after, and vice versa. This is puzzling. But it should be remembered that the effect only exists *net* of the presence of a large number of After-interaction terms in the model (including the 'regression-adjustment' term, explaining an ED's After risk by its Before risk). In the null model it is strongly positive. In effect, the predominant positive elements of the relationship between Before and After are represented elsewhere in the model, and what we have left is a residual negative relationship.

The *Level 2* random term represents between-respondent variation. The *Level 1* random term represents the residual unexplained variance between interviews. This was allowed to vary from a fixed value of 1 to reveal any extra-binomial variation. In fact the extra-binomial variation was not significant.

Taken together, the variation (and covariation) in the intercepts at Levels 1, 2 and 3 are equivalent to the residual, unexplained, variation in ordinary least squares regression. What has been achieved is a proper allocation of components of variation to each of the units within the hierarchy.

The variables/interactions, estimated coefficients and standard errors of the estimates are listed in Table A1.3

Table A1.3 Random components in survey model

VARIABLE IN MODEL	COEFFICIENT ESTIMATE	STANDARD ERROR
LEVEL 3 (Areas: 1981 Census Enumeration Districts, n = 406)		
Constant, for Before interviews, between-area variance	0.1499	0.08233
Constant, for After interviews, between-area variance	0.008842	0.0746
Before/After, between-area covariance	-0.1361	0.05788
LEVEL 2 (Respondents, n = 5,835)		
Constant, for all interviews, between-respondent variance	1.075	0.2238
LEVEL 1 (Interviews, n = 7,679)		
Constant, for all interviews, residual between-interview variance	0.8962	0.02336

Significance testing

The *goodness of fit* statistic, or likelihood, in multilevel modelling measures how closely the *model* predicts the *observed* values of burglary risk over all interviews. Significance testing of a particular explanatory term (variable) is based on comparing the fit of models with, and without that term, to the observed data, and examining the relative reduction (if any) in the likelihood.

It is easier, presentationally, to work backwards from the full model and show the *decrement in the fit* obtained when particular terms are removed from the model. The model contained four terms representing Safer Cities after-effects (shown at the very end of Table A1.2 – general step and marginal after-effects, and their respective subsidiary interactions with prior burglary risk). The *subsidiary interactions* – the respective terms for the interactions of the step and marginal-intensity effects with prior burglary risk were removed before their respective general term. (If the *subsidiary* interaction for the step effect, say, was left in when the *general* step effect was removed, this would underestimate the decrement in fit due to the step effect – because the interaction would now 'stand in' for part of the general step effect.)

The test results presented are those in which all other terms are in the model – for example, the extra contribution to fit of the step effect is tested with the marginal-intensity effect already present, and vice versa. (The *locational* effects of action remain in the whole time – filtering out the overall effect on burglary risk of where the co-ordinators happened to locate the action.) Otherwise the tests would have been too generous because of any correlation between the different Safer Cities effect terms. For example, the presence of action was, obviously, correlated with the amount of action: removing the marginal term with the step term already taken out would have given the marginal term a greater than merited decrement in fit, because it would have been partially standing in for the step term.

The tests may be somewhat over-generous because the multi-level modelling was unable to take account of *all* design effects due, for example, to clustering of EDs in the co-ordinator-identified survey set. However, the significance levels of the terms representing the Safer Cities effects were in most cases high enough to give reasonable leeway. The confidence limits around the estimates of the impact of action on risk were, though, extremely wide (as the standard errors in the above list show). As might be expected, there was much variation in the impact of what were quite a diverse collection of schemes implemented in a variety of contexts. *Therefore, the estimates should be regarded as a sound quantitative guide to the presence/absence of an effect, rather than being taken too literally.*

The results of removing particular terms from the model are shown in Figure A1.1. The fit statistic is calculated as -2[log(likelihood ratio)]. Larger (strictly, more positive) numbers indicate a *poorer* fit – in other words, less of the observed variation in risk is predicted or explained by the model. The decrement in fit is approximately distributed as Chi-squared (with degrees of freedom = number of terms dropped).

Figure A1.1 Statistical significance of Safer Cities after-effects

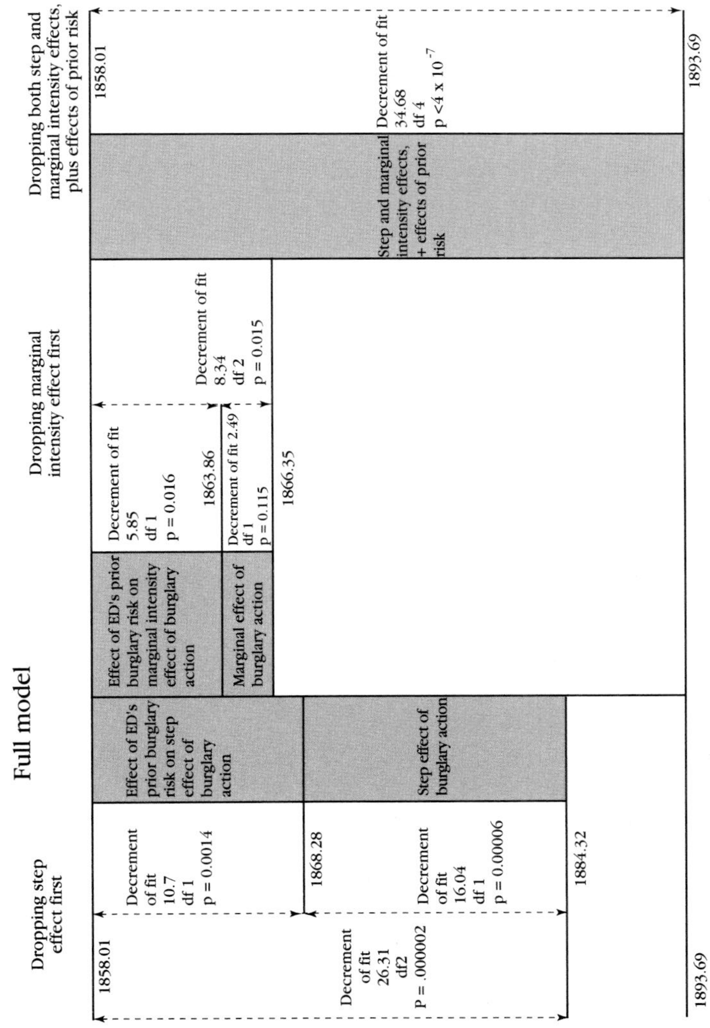

The full model as a whole is tested against a 'null model', a highly cut-down version which in this case comprises:

Fixed terms: Intercept for all interviews
                    After indicator

Random terms: Level 1 (residual between-interview) variation of intercept
                    Level 2 (between-respondents) variation of intercept
                    Level 3 (between-EDs) variation of Before intercept term
                    Level 3 (between-EDs) variation of After intercept term Level 3 Before-After (between-ED) covariance

The difference in the likelihood comparing the full model to the base/null model showed a decrement of *1424.21*, 77 df (p <<*0.00001*), derived from *3282.22*, 7df (null) minus *1858.01*, 84 df (full).

Generating expected values for display: Sample enumeration

The presentation of results in Figures 2.3 and 2.4 is based on a technique called 'sample enumeration' (Davies, 1992a,b). (This is nothing to do with survey sampling.) The central aim is to generate the 'counterfactual' – values of burglary risk in the after survey in the action areas, which we would have *expected* to find had there been no action, but everything else remained the same. 'Everything else' means common background trends and between-area differences. Generating expected values involves several steps:

i)   generating predicted (i.e. expected) burglary risk values (in logistic form, i.e. logeodds) for every interview in the after-survey, based on all explanatory variables in the entire fixed statistical model as in Table A1.2

ii)   generating for every after-interview, the 'logeodds multiplier' from the values of the terms representing the after-effects of Safer Cities action (both step and marginal intensity effects and their interactions with prior burglary risk)

iii) subtracting the latter from the former to leave the expected (logeodds) burglary risk (expected on the basis of all terms other than those representing the Safer Cities after-effect) for each after-interview

iv) transforming this to prevalence probability risk values

v)   averaging this value over each surveyed ED to produce the expected after-burglary prevalence probability risk for each ED

vi) subtracting the expected ED risk from the ED average observed risk, to produce the 'observed - expected' prevalence probability risk for each ED (O-E thus amounts to our estimate of the Safer Cities effect *plus* the residual, unexplained variation)

vii) calculating relative percentage change (RPC) as

$$\frac{100\ [\text{observed - expected}]}{\text{expected}}$$

viii) then averaging observed ED burglary risks over each of the 'action sets' of EDS – low, middle and high action; doing likewise for expected risks and RPC.

It is these latter grouped averages that are presented in the figures. We averaged to ED first (step v) before averaging again to these groups of EDs, because EDs were our focal unit of analysis, and we did not want to weight the grouped averages by the number of interviews in each ED.

The relationship between RPC and (low, medium and high) action intensity levels in Figure 2.4 illustrates the Safer Cities effect estimated in our model, under the particular conditions measured for each respondent, and for each ED. As stated in step vi), it also incorporates the variation unexplained in the model.

Figure A1.2 shows the same relationship of RPC with action intensity, but this time plotted on an individual ED basis for the 117 action EDs. Also on the figure is a simple linear OLS regression line showing both the step down and the less reliable downward slope of the marginal intensity effect identified in the model. Removing the extreme values of the action intensity scores above £100/household made virtually no difference to the line. It would be interesting to compare the anti-burglary action in EDs falling significantly below this line (i.e. performing better than average) with those above it (i.e. performing worse than average).

*Figure A1.2 Survey: relative percentage change in burglary
prevalence for each action ED, against action intensity*

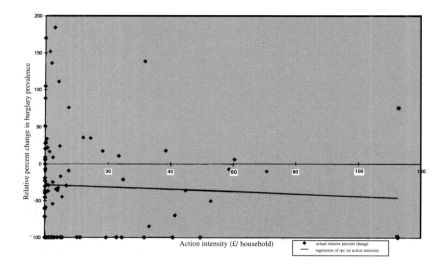

Note: Four points with zero action and extreme RPCs were omitted for scaling purposes

Calculating the estimated reductions in risk due to burglary action

The step effect

In the statistical model, our starting point was the regression coefficient associated with the term representing the presence of Safer Cities action (a dichotomous variable). The value of this coefficient (-0.293, found near the bottom of Table A1.2) was the reduction in risk, associated with the presence of action, of $\log_e$(odds of victimisation/non-victimisation). Transforming this to the reduction in probability of victimisation involved several steps.

Calculating the simple step effect

1) Taking a sample prevalence probability (*The 10% row, 3rd down in Table A1.4*)	sample probability of burglary prevalence per household in one year = 10% or 0.1
2) Converting probability to odds	sample odds = p/(1-p) = 10%/90% = 0.1111
3) Taking the log$_e$ transform of this	log$_e$ (sample odds) = log$_e$ (0.111) = -2.1972
4) Adding the 'step' coefficient to this (being a negative number, it reduced the risk) to adjust the transformed odds by the step effect	adjusted transformed odds = -2.1972 + (-0.293) = -2.4902
5) Transforming the adjusted transformed odds back in the reverse direction:	
5.1) Raising e to the value of the sum	adjusted odds = $e^{(-2.4902)}$ = 0.083
5.2) Dividing (e to the value of the sum) by (1+(e to the value of the sum)) to convert odds back to probability	adjusted probability = 0.083/(1+0.083) = 0.0765
6) Subtracting the adjusted probability from the original sample value, to give the absolute reduction in prevalence probability associated with the presence of action	absolute reduction in prevalence probability associated with the presence of action = 0.1 - 0.0765 = 0.0235
7) Dividing the absolute reduction in probability by the original sample probability, and multiplying by 100, to give the percent reduction in probability of a households' victimisation at least once in a year	**percent reduction in probability of burglary victimisation due to step effect of burglary action, at prior burglary probability of 10%** = (0.0235/0.1) x100 = **23.5%**

Taking account of the influence of the prior burglary probability on the step reduction involved a further stage. This interaction of step effect and prior burglary probability was also represented as a term in the model (derived by multiplying prior burglary probability in an ED x presence of action in that ED x After dummy), and was assigned its own regression coefficient. Instead of adding just the step coefficient to the transformed sample prevalence risk, we also added the step interaction coefficient (the special effect of prior burglary probability on step, -0.8283) x the sample prevalence probability (10%).

Repeating the example from step 4), with the the effect of the prior burglary probability on the Safer Cities step effect included, gives:

Calculating the step effect taking account of prior burglary risk

4) Adding to the transformed sample odds: a) the 'step' coefficient, plus b) (the step interaction coefficient x the sample prevalence probability) to adjust the transformed odds by the step effect and its interaction with prior burglary probability	adjusted transformed odds = -2.1972 + (-0.293) + (0.1 x (-0.8283)) =-2.573
5) Transforming the adjusted transformed odds back in reverse direction. 5.1) Raising e to the value of the sum	adjusted odds = $e^{(-2.573)}$ = 0.0763
5.2) Dividing (e to the value of the sum) by (1 + (e to the value of sum)) to convert from odds back to probability	adjusted probability = 0.0763 / (1 + 0.0763) = 0.0709
6) Subtracting the adjusted probability from the original sample probability, to give the absolute reduction in prevalence probability associated with the presence of action	absolute reduction in prevalence probability associated with the presence of action = 0.1 - 0.0709 = 0.0291
7) Dividing the absolute reduction in probability by the original sample probability, and multiplying by 100, to give the percent reduction in probability of a households' victimisation at least once in the year *(entered in row 3, column 2 of Table A1.4)*	**percent reduction in probability of burglary victimisation due to step effect of burglary action, at prior burglary probability of 10%, and taking account of special effect of prior burglary risk on step** = (0.0291 / 0.1) x 100 = **29.1%**

We thus estimate that at a prior burglary prevalence probability of 10%, the adjusted prevalence probability is 7.1 per cent, and the reduction in this probability due to the step effect is just over 29 per cent. Likewise, starting with a prior probability of 5 per cent, the adjusted prevalence probability is 3.65 per cent, a reduction of 27 per cent. The rest of Table A1.4 was completed in this way.

The overall effect

The *overall* effect of action on prevalence of burglary was calculated in a similar way to the step effect. The difference was, that to the sum of the transformed sample prevalence probability and the step effects, were added the marginal-intensity effect (a coefficient of -0.003 from the model) multiplied by a particular action score, and its interaction with prior burglary probability (a coefficient of + 0.01355). (These values are at the bottom of Table A1.2.) We used as an exemplary value the marginal reduction in probability associated with the *average action intensity of £16*. ('Average' intensity of action was taken as the mean, because we wanted to take account of the wide range of action intensities; median values were considerably lower, but made little difference to the cost estimates.) Taking account of the influence of the prior burglary probability on the marginal-intensity effect of action involved a process similar to that with the step effect. Altogether, the overall effect on the sample prior burglary prevalence probability is the combination of:

> the step effect plus its interaction with prior burglary prevalence probability
> + the marginal-intensity effect plus its interaction with prior burglary prevalence probability.

Calculating the overall effect taking account of prior burglary risk

1) Taking a sample prevalence probability (*Again from the 10% row in Table A1.4*	sample probability of burglary prevalence per household in 1 year $= 10\%$ or 0.1
2) Converting probability to odds	sample odds $= p/(1-p)$ $= 10\%/90\%$ $= 0.1111$
3) Taking the $\log_e$ transform of this	$\log_e$ (sample odds) $= \log_e (0.111)$ $= -2.1972$
4) Adding to the transformed sample odds (-2.1972): a) the 'step' coefficient (-0.293), plus b) the step interaction coefficient (-0.8283) x the sample prevalence probability (0.1) c) the marginal coefficient (-0.003) x the sample amount of action (£16) d) the marginal interaction coefficient (0.1355) x the sample amount action (£16) x the sample prevalence probability (0.1) to adjust the transformed odds by the step effect and marginal–intensity effect, and heir interactions with prior burglary probability	adjusted transformed odds $= -2.1972 +$ $= (-0.293) + (-0.8283)$ $+ \ (-0.003 \times 16) +$ $(0.01355 \times 16 \times 0.1)$ $= -2.5994$
5) Transforming the adjusted transformed odds back in the reverse direction: a) Raising e to the value of the sum b) Dividing (e to the value of the sum) by (1 + (e to the value of the sum).to convert from odds back to probability	adjusted odds $= e^{(-2.5994)}$ $= 0.0743$ adjusted probability $= 0.0743 /$ $(1 + 0.0743)$ $= 0.0692$
6) Subtracting the adjusted probability from the original sample probability, to give the absolute reduction in prevalence probability associated with the presence of action	absolute reduction in prevalence probability associated with the presence of action $= 0.1 - 0.0692$ $= 0.0308$
7) Dividing the absolute reduction in probability by the original sample probability and multiplying by 100, to give the percent reduction in probability (*entered as 31% in row 3, column 4 of Table A1.4*)	**percent reduction in probability of burglary victimisation due to step and marginal–intensity effects of burglary action, at average action intensity of £16 and prior burglary probability of 10%, and taking account of special effects of prior burglary probability on step and marginal** $= (0.0308/0.1) \times 100$ $= 30.8\%$

The marginal–intensity effect

The regression coefficient for the marginal-intensity effect represented the effect of an extra £1 worth of action, rather than merely the presence of action. But in estimating the real-world value of the marginal-intensity effect, we could not simply calculate from the marginal-intensity effect coefficient alone – the non-linear (logarithmic) relationship within the model meant we had to work with the overall effect (i.e. step + marginal coefficients combined). Therefore, to produce a representative estimate for our illustration:

> We calculated the reduction in risk associated
> i) with the average action intensity of £16 (as above), and then
> ii) repeated the calculation for £17. The difference in the reduction in risk between these two estimates was the *marginal-intensity effect of an extra £1 per household.*

> At a prevalence of 10%, this gave a marginal reduction of probability of burglary of *0.11% for an extra £1 of Safer Cities burglary action per household.*

Repeating this calculation for, say, £16 and £26 gave the marginal reduction associated with an extra £10. A marginal reduction in risk derived from a *£10* increase in action was about *17* times the marginal reduction from a £1 increase – so there appeared (within limits) to be proportionally better returns from bigger investments. On the other hand, a similar analysis with the recorded crime model showed diminishing returns. However, it is not known without further exploration whether these are real-world relationships, or merely peculiarities of the statistical models and the transformations necessary to meet the requirements of statistical testing.

These calculations – step, overall and marginal – were repeated for a range of sample burglary risks (Table A1.4). The same exercise was also carried out using the model which distinguished between burglary action alone, and burglary action plus other Safer Cities action. The figures in brackets are the results. Here, the four 'burglary-plus' coefficients substituted for the 'burglary-general' ones used in the above examples. There was an additional term added to the others in stage 5): the 'joint action multiplier', whose coefficient was multiplied by the amount of burglary action x the amount of other action. This slightly increased the adjusted and transformed odds.

Table A1.4 Survey results – Reductions in burglary prevalence risk associated with Safer Cities action against burglary (all burglary action, and action accompanied by other Safer Cities action)

Prior burglary prevalence %	Step percentage reduction in risk due to **presence** of burglary action [and in presence of other action]	Marginal percentage reduction in risk **per extra £** of burglary action [and in presence of other action]	Overall percentage reduction in risk [and in presence of other action]
3	27 [17]	0.18 [0.61]	30 [25]
5	27 [17]	0.16 [0.60]	30 [24]
10	29 [16]	0.11 [0.57]	31 [23]
15	31 [15]	0.06 [0.54]	32 [22]
20	32 [14]	0.02 [0.51]	32 [20]
25	32 [13]	- [0.47]	33 [19]
30	33 [12]	- [0.44]	33 [18]
35	34 [11]	- [0.41]	33 [16]

Note: the reductions are estimated relative to the expected probability in the *after* survey, in the absence of Safer Cities action. (They are not proportional falls from the *prior* burglary probability.) Figures in *brackets* are from EDs where burglary is accompanied by other action, and are less reliable. The 3% burglary prevalence probability is the national average from the British Crime Survey; the 10% probability is the average from the present survey. The action input comprises both Safer Cities and levered funds.

The *step* effect is the reduction in probability associated simply with the presence of Safer Cities action in the relevant ED in the year of the after-survey. The *overall* effect is the reduction in probability associated with the presence of Safer Cities burglary action in an ED, at the average intensity of £16.00 per household over the year preceeding the after-survey. The *marginal* effect is the further reduction in probability for an extra £1 of action per household, beyond £16, spent in the ED at the time of original implementation.

Cost effectiveness calculations from the survey findings

Calculating the overall and marginal costs of preventing one (and one more) burglary involved using the relevant coefficients in the model, and feeding in a number of additional assumptions about key quantities such as the two-year duration of impact.

The overall cost

Estimating the overall cost involved several steps. We begin with the absolute reduction in prevalence probability risk associated with the presence and amount of action, taking account of the special effect of prior burglary probability. This is 0.0308 in step 6) of the last example above, with prior burglary (prevalence) probability at 10%, and average Safer Cities burglary action amounting to £16 per household-year. *Italic* figures in [brackets] in the right-hand column are example calculations for *'burglary-plus'* action which were ultimately preferred for comparability with the recorded crime estimates (although much less reliable), for reasons given in the main text. Our careful definition of the amount (intensity) of action, as *the average input of scheme funds per household in the ED over the year of measurement,* enabled us to link the coefficient back to real-world cost values.

Overall cost calculations:

a) Taking the absolute reduction in prevalence probability per household, over the year of measurement, previously calculated for the overall effect
(step 6, 'overall reduction in risk calculations', using reductions estimated for 10% prior burglary prevalence probability)

absolute reduction in prevalence probability per household
= 0.0308
 [= 0.02298]

b) Assuming for the purpose of calculation that the average amount of SC burglary action was present (£16 per household–year); and that this was accompanied by £7 of other SC action, making a total of £23

total SC action present per household–year
= £16 SC burglary + £7 SC other
 [= £11.50 + £8.76]
= £23
 [=£20.26]

c) Say £23 present per household over a year, x 100 households, causes 3.08 fewer households burgled that year and costs £2,300. The cost per burglary prevented is £2,300 / 3.08 i.e. £747. (The year factor cancels out as at this point all calculations are based on one year.

basic overall cost per burglary prevented
= (average intensity of SC burglary action + average intensity of SC other action) x
(1 / reduction in prevalence probability for action of that intensity,
= £23 / 0.0308 = £747
 [= £20.26 / 0.02298 = £881]

d) Adjust basic overall cost to take account of impact duration (assumed 2 years), overheads (£1.50 total spend every £1 spent on schemes), and 1.5 incidents prevented per victimised household prevented *(£441 entered as 'about £400' in Part 2 'What sort of money does one have to spend to prevent a burglary?', and as £441 on the 'overall cost' line in Figure 4.1a)*

adjusted overall cost per burglaryt prevented
= basic cost x 1/2 x 1.5 / 1.5
= £373
 [= £441]

note: [£441] is estimate for burglary-plus action

The marginal cost

The marginal cost is how much *more* money needed to be invested in an area, at the time the action was originally implemented, to prevent *one more burglary*. The marginal cost of preventing one extra burglary was estimated in a similar way to the overall cost, with a few exceptions:

i)   Step a) began with the difference between the reductions of probability for 1) the burglary action of average intensity (£16 for general estimate, £11.50 for burglary-plus estimate), and 2) the burglary action of £1 greater intensity (£17 and £12.50 respectively). These were probability reductions of 0.00011 and *0.0005694 (Table A1.4 value of 0.57 was rounded)* respectively

ii) Step b) was omitted

iii) These reductions were inverted as in step c), but not multiplied by the total (burglary action + SC other action) intensity. Instead,

iv) For the calculation of the marginal-intensity effect of burglary-plus action, every extra pound of Safer Cities burglary action was also accompanied by a certain average amount of extra other action. So in step d) we further multiplied the 'marginal pound' by

$$\frac{\textit{average burglary action intensity} + \textit{average other action intensity}}{\textit{average burglary action intensity}}$$

in these areas, i.e.

$$\frac{£11.50 + £8.76}{£11.50} \quad or \quad 1.76$$

Thus the marginal cost calculations involved:

Marginal cost calculations

a) Taking the difference between the reductions of probability over the year of measuement, previously calculated for the overall effect for 1) the burglary action of average intensity (£16 for general estimate, *£11.50 for burglary-plus estimate*), and 2) the burglary action of £1 greater intensity (£17 and £12.50 respectively)

difference in absolute reduction in prevalence probability per household between (burglary action of average intensity) and (of average intensity + £1)

$$= 0.00011$$
$$[= 0.0005694]$$

c) Say an extra £1 present per household over a year, x 100 households, causes 0.011 (i.e., 100 x 0.00011) fewer households burgled that year and costs £100. The cost per extra burglary prevented is £100 / 0.011 i.e., £9,090. (The year factor cancels out as at this point all calculations are based on 1 year.)

basic marginal cost per extra burglary prevented
= (increase in intensity of SC burglary action)
x
(1 / reduction in prevalence probability for that increase in intensity)
$$= £1 / 0.00011 = £9,090$$
$$[= £1 / 0.0005694]$$
$$[£1,756]$$

d) Adjust basic marginal cost to take account of impact duration (assumed 2 years), overheads (£1.50 total spend for every £1 spent on schemes), 1.5 incidents prevented per victimised household prevented, *and ratio of (total action average intensity): (SC burglary action average intensity)*, 1.76

adjusted marginal cost per extra burglary prevented
= basic cost x 1/2 x 1.5 / 1.5
$$[x 1.76]$$
$$= £4,545$$
$$[= £1,545]$$

Note: [£1,545] is estimate for burglary-plus action

Appendix 2: In search of displacement in the surveyed EDs

This appendix provides further detail on the final look at geographic displacement, repeating and expanding the main text where appropriate.

We took account of any burglary action in the *ring* of EDs that surrounded each surveyed ED in the Safer Cities (the *'bullseye'*). This was 'extra' action only; it excluded schemes which covered both the surrounding neighbourhood and the surveyed ED itself. We reasoned that schemes which covered ring(s) and bullseye together would not shift crime from one to the other. Three 'extra adjacent action' scores were generated for each surveyed ED, to explore close-range and somewhat longer-range effects: i) burglary action in the *inner ring* of EDs immediately adjacent to the bullseye; ii) burglary action in an *outer ring* of EDs immediately outside the inner ring; and iii) a pooled score of burglary action in *either or both inner and outer rings*.

Generation of these rings was done using the geographic information system, aided by visual on-screen inspection of the rings the software generated, to remove anomalies. 1991 EDs were used as the basis. Where two or more surveyed 1991 EDs were clustered together (equivalent to a single surveyed 1981 ED), a common ring around the two of them was produced. As Figure A2.1 shows, the rings were extremely ragged, defined as they were by ED boundaries. The EDs themselves were also very variable in size, meaning that action in the inner ring was only *on average* closer to the surveyed ED of the bullseye.

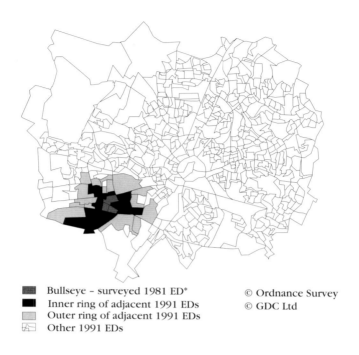

Bullseye – surveyed 1981 ED*
Inner ring of adjacent 1991 EDs
Outer ring of adjacent 1991 EDs
Other 1991 EDs

© Ordnance Survey
© GDC Ltd

*The surveyed 1981 ED illustrated was split into three 1991 EDs

We then distinguished between our surveyed EDs on the basis of whether or
not they had burglary action in the bullseye, and whether or not they had
extra burglary action in the various surrounding rings. There were seven
distinct geographical patterns:

(a)   Action in *bullseye* alone

(b)   Action in *bullseye* and extra action in *inner ring* only

(c)   Action in *bullseye* and extra action in *outer ring* only

(d)   Action in *bullseye* and extra action in *both rings*

(e)   No action in bullseye but extra action in *inner ring* only

(f)   No action in bullseye but extra action in *outer ring* only

(g)   No action in bullseye but extra action in *both rings*.

Of the 280 surveyed EDs in the Safer Cities, 109 had extra burglary action in
one or other or both rings (a further 104 had action neither in rings nor
bullseye). The respective 'extra, adjacent action' scores were incorporated
in slightly simplified versions of the existing statistical model.

Technical problems make it difficult to estimate the statistical significance of the component adjacent action scores in the model. In many cases, particularly in the smaller cities and boroughs surveyed, the bullseye of one surveyed ED also comprises part of the ring of another. This means that the assumption of independence of the areas sampled is violated. This may be connected with the observation that incorporating 'extra adjacent action' scores in the statistical models in most cases actually worsens the fit slightly. They must therefore be used as diagnostic clues rather than firm findings. They can be understood in terms of the preventive 'Safer Cities effect' plus several additional processes: *displacement, diffusion of benefit, deflection* (plus *security enveloping* and *synergy), distance* and *depth.*

Table A2.1 presents, for each of the geographical patterns, the amounts of various kinds of *action present in the bullseye and rings,* and the *changes in burglary risk in the bullseye* that are associated with the action. (These are the numbers behind Table 2.3 in the main text.) We were unable to measure risk in the rings themselves – only in the bullseye. To simplify the steps in the calculation, we present reductions in risk in the *odds* of burglary victimisation rather than in the probability. At or below the average burglary risk in the survey (10% prevalence probability), the results from the odds are close to the results from the probability.

As with the main analysis, we have to distinguish between the effects of the *presence* of action (in the bullseye and/or in the relevant ring) and the marginal-intensity effects of the *amount* (again, in the bullseye and/or in the relevant ring). This is particularly necessary because, as rows 2 to 4 of the table show, the geographical patterns have quite different amounts of action. (Simply modelling presence (step) effects to reduce the complexity of the analysis would therefore give arbitrary results.) Moreover, as will be seen, in some circumstances the amount and the presence of action exert *opposing* influences on risk.

Table A2.1 Changes in burglary risk ‡ associated with various geographical patterns of action

		Geographical patterns of burglary action						
		Action **present** in bullseye and extra action:				Action **absent** in bullseye and extra action:		
		(a) Nowhere else	**(b)** Inner ring only ⌖	**(c)** Outer ring only	**(d)** Both rings	**(e)** Inner ring only	**(f)** Outer ring only	**(g)** Both rings
No. surveyed EDs	1	67	3	19	28	22	22	15
SC **burglary** action in **bullseye** £/hhd yr	2	20	2	6	15	---	---	---
Other SC action in **bullseye** £/hhd yr	3	4	1	10	13	<1	<1	2
Extra adjacent **burglary** action in **ring/s** £/hhd yr	4	---	21	2	2	4	1	3
Step % change in risk due to mere presence of action in **bullseye** (net of amount)	5	-9%	*			-	-	-
Marginal % change in risk due to £1 action in **bullseye** (net of presence of action)	6	-1%	+2%○			-	-	-
Step % change in risk due to mere presence of action in relevant **ring** and/or **bullseye** (net of amounts)	7	-	[-35%]	-10%	-66%	+38%	+8%	+112%
Marginal % change in risk due to £1 extra action in **ring** (net of presence of action)	8	-	[+48%]	-3%	-2%	-7%	-4%	-20%
Marginal % change in risk due to **joint action** - £1 in **ring** and £1 in **bullseye** (net of presence of action)	9	-	[-9%]	-17%	0%	-	-	-
Overall % change in risk at £1 extra action in **ring**, plus £1 action in **bullseye**§	10	-10%	[-11%]	-27%	-66%	+33%	+4%	+69%
Overall % change in risk at £1 extra action in **ring**, plus £10 action in **bullseye**§	11	-15%	[-56%]	-84%	-59%	+33%	+4%	+69%
Overall % change in risk at £10 extra action in **ring**, plus £1 action in **bullseye**§	12	-10%	[+1200%]	-90%	-72%	-33%	-26%	-78%
Overall % change in risk at £10 extra action in **ring**, plus ·£10 action in **bullseye**§	13	-15%	[-99%]	-99%	-65%	-33%	-26%	-78%

‡ Risk is the odds of burglary victimisation (prevalence) in each surveyed ED; change in risk is the % reduction in the odds of victimisation specific to the **after** survey, associated with the presence and/or amount of the relevant type/s of action.

✱ Effects of presence of action in bullseye are measured **jointly** with presence of extra action in ring, which appear in other cells – so do not appear seperately here.

§ In some cells, where only one type of action is present, the overall change is calculated from the step and marginal–intensity effects of bullseye action only, or of ring action only.

⌖ Since there are only 3 EDs in this set, the results are particularly unreliable although they are mostly consistent with the pattern in the other sets; the large marginal increase in risk per £1 extra in the ring may be attributed to sampling error and/or the very high amount of action in the inner ring coupled with low burglary and other action in the bullseye.

○ The marginal **increase** with the amount of action in the bullseye, with adjacent action present (row 6) opposes the main Safer Cities effect – the **decrease** in risk has in most cases been taken up by the interaction with the extra adjacent action (row 9), or in the step effects of the joint presence of action in the bullseye and the rings (row 7).

Rows 5-9 of the table show the estimated influence on risk of various specific *components* of the action. Rows 10-13 show the overall influence on risk of the *combined effects* of these components, under low and high intensities of action in the bullseye and in the rings. (On a precautionary note, in interpreting these patterns we assume a homogeneity of effects across the schemes covered, with all differences observed being due merely to geography. This may not necessarily be so. Some schemes may have focussed on areas, while others targetted individual victims of crime: an uneven distribution may have confounded the purely geographical patterns, but this was not explored.)

Displacement seems to be shown in columns (e) to (g) where there is no action in the bullseye. The *step* effects (row 7) show a clear *increase* in risk in the bullseye when extra action is present close by. However, this is not the whole story, because the marginal-intensity effects (row 8) operate in the reverse direction. The *more* the action, the more the increase in risk due to the presence of adjacent action is *eroded*. It is possible that two processes are occurring. First, offenders may be relocating their efforts in the light of knowledge that 'something has been done to enhance household security' in their favoured area. This may merely drive them to the immediately adjacent streets. Second, higher intensities of action may put them off altogether, especially if they are unsure of the boundaries of the action. Given that they may be unwilling to travel greater distances and/or to unfamiliar territory, this may have served to produce a real drop in offending. Since the drop appears to cover an area wider than the intended territory of the scheme, the falls (in row 8, (e) to (g)) may be evidence for *Diffusion of benefit.*

Deflection is shown in columns (b) – (d) of the table, which represent the effects of action in the bullseye and the rings together. Under these conditions (action in the inner ring plus bullseye), the extra adjacent action reduces the risk in the bullseye, with the partial exception of column (b). There were, however, only three surveyed EDs with bullseye action, plus extra action in the inner ring alone. This renders these results particularly unreliable. The high amount of extra adjacent action, together with the unusually low amounts of burglary action and other action in the bullseye may also have been responsible for the extreme and sometimes anomalous effects displayed. This is true for both presence and amount of adjacent action (step and marginal-intensity effects, rows 7 and 8). What seems to be happening is that under the joint influence of action in the rings and in the bullseye, offenders are inhibited, or deflected elsewhere. Action in the bullseye may be protecting it from inward displacement from neighbouring schemes. The different burglary schemes located in the ring and the bullseye in effect may link up to provide one common territory which is unattractive to burglars. This could be called *'security enveloping'*.

Furthermore, there appears to be a real *synergistic* effect – in some cases there is an extra (marginal) risk-reducing effect of the amount of *joint* action (row 9, (c)). The overall reduction thus is greater than the sum of the reductions from the two types of action taken individually. (This joint term is the multiplicative interaction of the amount of action in the bullseye and the amount of extra action in the relevant ring(s). It is additional to the term representing the amount of action in the ring and the mere presence of action in the bullseye, (row 8, (c).) However, this pattern is not completely consistent (row 9, (d) is zero where we might have expected the strongest joint reduction effect).

Prevention appears in column (a). The EDs with action in the *bullseye* but *no extra adjacent action* show the Safer Cities effect: the usual pattern of reductions of risk associated with the presence (step, row 5) and the amount (marginal-intensity effect, row 6) of action. The step effect for these 70 EDs is weaker than the overall step effect for all 120 EDs with action (9% reduction in odds of victimisation versus 25% in the main model, not shown in this table). This suggests that the overall step effect was boosted by deflection from adjacent action – the 'security enveloping' already mentioned.

Distance of action from the point of measurement would be expected to play a part, given offenders' propensity to minimise effort and risk by staying in familiar territory (Brantingham and Brantingham, 1991). Distance effects can in fact be seen in noting the weaker influence on risk of the outer rings (columns (c) and (f)) compared with the inner rings (columns (b) and (e)). The step reduction in risk with action in the bullseye plus the outer ring (10%, in row 7, column (c)) is close to the reduction with action in the bullseye alone (9%, in row 5, column (a)). It is possible that the bulk of the influence of action in the outer rings was felt in the inner ring, or further out still beyond the outer ring.

It is plausible that burglars will be more strongly influenced by action that protects a wider territory. This will offer less reward per distance covered (i.e. effort) and may present greater risks in longer exposure going equipped to a burglary or returning with booty from a burglary, over less-familiar territory. This could be called the *depth* of the 'hinterland of action'. Depth effects are most prominent in the two patterns where adjacent action covers more than one ring (columns (d) and (g), rows 7 and 8), although this wider coverage may not always be from the one scheme. With or without action in the bullseye, and in whichever direction the effect goes (increasing or reducing risk), the change in risk is mostly greater than where action covers one ring only.

When these influences are combined (in rows 10–13 of the table), we can see clearly that the burglary action in the bullseye and the extra adjacent action in the rings are working together to reduce the risk in the bullseye, often to a substantial degree (columns (b) to (d)). When there is no action in the bullseye, the *direction* of the effect of extra adjacent action depends on the amount (columns (e) to (g)). With *low* amounts of adjacent action, the step effect prevails and there is an overall *increase* in risk in the bullseye. With *high* amounts of adjacent action, the marginal-intensity effect prevails and there is an overall *decrease* in risk in the bullseye. In these circumstances, the more intense action may have driven offenders further off, caused them to switch to other targets, or forced them to give up altogether.

Appendix 3:The statistical model for the recorded crime data: explaining variation in risk of burglary incidence

Multilevel-models

Multilevel models are explained in Appendix 1. In the analysis of the recorded crime data, our interest is in the following levels: *beat-years, beats* and (originally) *cities*. The second and third levels are groupings of beat-years in a hierarchy. It is at the beat-year level that we measured the amount of Safer Cities action present, and we looked for its special effects on burglary risk. Since there are up to six beat-year observations within each beat, this is a 'repeated measures' model. The multilevel approach takes account of the relatedness of these observations, which would cause under-estimation of standard errors in ordinary least squares regression. The outcome measure (dependent variable) had to be transformed in order to remove negative skew in the frequency distribution of incidence risks – many beat-years had very low values. Comparison city incidence risks were included as *explanatory* variables (and transformed in the same way as the dependent variable). This contrasted with the survey model, where burglary victimisation in both comparison cities and Safer Cities were treated together as the *dependent* variable.

Table A3.1 Recorded crime model parameters

Dependent variable: burglary incidence per household
Transformation: arcsine of 4th root

Hierarchy	Units of analysis	
Level 3:	City*	N = 14 (all Safer Cities)
Level 2:	Beat/superbeat	N = 701
Level 1:	Beat-year (max 6 yrs)**	N = 3,277

*City level was subsequently omitted from models. This was due to reduction in the unexplained between-cities variance of the intercept. The reduction resulted from incorporation of city-level explanatory variables.

**Not all beats were available for all years as described in the main text.

Taking account of time and trend

Static and dynamic locational effects are described in the main text reflecting the properties of beats where Safer Cities action happened to be sited. With the dynamic locational effects, more strictly speaking the relevant trend terms in the statistical model reflected the *special* effect on burglary risk of being in Safer Cities action beats, beyond and above the *general* trend relationship common to all beats. For example, there was a general term in the model reflecting any trend over time common to all beats; the term reflecting the special time trend of just the action beats, represented any net differences these may have had from the general trend.

With the comparison city indicators, we took separate account of the global and city Census family versions.

Additional biases could have come from any tendency for action to be located in beats with an incomplete series of six years' records, or in superbeats. The static and dynamic locational effects of action beats already described were further split to take account of these possibilities. The 'incomplete records' problem was especially difficult as it left us with some beats which had no 'tail' of records before action began – although the proportion of affected cases was fairly small. (Of the 326 beats with action, only 55 had no tail in this way, all but eight in the 'low' action band. Of 734 action beat-years, 124 were from beats which had no tail.) Here, we could not use any terms in the model which distinguished between the 'after-effect' of action, and the locational effect of being in a beat where action eventually occurred. To allow these beats to contribute to the locational effect of action would have unfairly weakened our chance of detecting a true Safer Cities effect, as any fall in burglary risk they may have shown would have been attributed to location, not action itself; but to eliminate them from the model altogether would have wasted data. The solution was to include them, without allowing them to contribute to the locational effect of action, but to see whether the Safer Cities effect itself in these curtailed beats was any different from that in the majority which were measured over all six years. (The results of this manoeuvre appear in Table A3.2 and are described in the note at its foot.)

Explanatory variables: Fixed components

A *positive* coefficient estimate for a fixed component indicates that the variable is associated with an *increased* risk of burglary victimisation; a *negative* estimate is associated with a *reduced* risk. The coefficient adjusts the predicted transformed risk, namely [Arcsine (burglary recorded incidence risk per household)$^{-4}$]. Cross-level interactions are listed under the relevant variables for which they are a subsidiary effect; they are indicated by, for example, L2/L1.

Police beats (and superbeats) usually bore no relationship to other administrative territories such as wards or EDs. In order to produce beat-level data for the analysis from the Census or the Index of Local Conditions, we had to digitise the beat/superbeat boundaries from beat maps, then 'tile' the beat territories with the smaller EDs whose boundaries we had purchased. This involved using the Geographic Information System and supplementing an automated routine with visual inspection of borderline cases. An example overlay of one beat and its constituent EDs is in Figure A3.1.

Figure A3.1 Overlay of 1991 EDs by police beat boundary

⊞ Other EDs	© Ordnance Survey
■ EDs overlapping one police beat	© GDC Ltd

The model (and the data on which it is based) has been specially designed for evaluation purposes. Therefore, the relationships, listed in Table A3.2 below, between the various explanatory variables and burglary risk should not be taken as representative of the country as a whole.

Table A3.2 Fixed components in recorded crime model

VARIABLE IN MODEL	COEFFICIENT ESTIMATE	STANDARD ERROR
Constant (common to all levels)	-5.568	1.045
LEVEL 1 (BEAT-YEAR) COMPONENTS		
Level 1 dynamic trends		
Year trend (1987 = 1) (L1)	0.001528	0.002401
...special trend for superbeats (L1/L2)*	0.007404	0.00472
...special trend for beats with incomplete series (L1/L2)*	0.07019	0.01271
Comparison cities trend – global (transformed) (L1)	0.4278	0.1194
...special trend for superbeats (L1/L2)*	0.1897	0.4678
...special trend for beats with incomplete series (L1/L2)	-1.212	0.8402
Comparison cities trend – by 1981 Census family (transformed) (L1)	0.4775	0.257
...special trend for superbeats (L1/L2)*	0.06385	0.1312
...special trend for beats with incomplete series (L1/L2)	-0.921	0.2312

*main model failed to converge with these terms in – but their inclusion made virtually no difference to estimates of Safer City effects. Values for these terms only are from this extended model

LEVEL 2 (BEAT) COMPONENTS		
L2 Beat selection/definition		
Beats with incomplete beat-years (<6 observations)	0.4925	0.3523
Superbeats	0.009313	0.01457
L2 Geographical data		
City centre beat (definition from local police)	-0.01487	0.01541
Beat area (Hectares)	-0.00004346	8.97×10^{-6}
Household density (calculated from Census and beat area)	0.0009392	0.0003281
L2 1991 ED Census percentages (converted to beat boundaries)		
% Black popn	-0.0004338	0.0003439
% Single parent hhold	-0.0003748	0.0003461
% Hhold without car	-0.0005634	0.0005349
% Unemployed popn	0.0005015	0.0009557
% One person hhold	-0.0003057	0.0006448
% Over 60 popn	-0.001903	0.0006592
% Young people 16–24	0.001273	0.001437
L2 1991 Index of Local Conditions, Beat level (from ED data)		
Overall Index	0.01894	0.004659
Overcrowding (> 1 person per room)	-0.007552	0.01436
Children in unsuitable accommodation	-0.008799	0.007408
Children in low-earning households	-0.01864	0.01155

Continued

Table A3.2 Fixed components in recorded crime model cont.

VARIABLE IN MODEL	COEFFICIENT ESTIMATE	STANDARD ERROR
LEVEL 3 (CITY) COMPONENTS		
L3 city selection: 1981 Census family groups		
(London groups = baseline)		
Census family 3	0.1561	0.07385
Census family 4a	0.2489	0.06081
Census family 4b	-2.194	0.4147
L3 Index of Local Conditions, Local Authority District level		
Low educational (GCSE) attainment	-0.3165	0.06217
Unemployment	-2.603	0.4813
Overcrowding (> 1 person per room)	-0.5266	0.09759
Residents in households lacking basic amenities	-0.3309	0.06226
Lack of educational participation (17–yr–olds not in full time education	0.00841	0.03129
Households with no car	2.325	0.3924
Standardised mortality rate	-1.942	0.3335
Ratio of long-term (> 1yr) to all unemployed	-0.3822	0.08149
Proportion of adults on income support	1.384	0.2656
Children in low-earning households	1.077	0.2468

SAFER CITIES ACTION COMPONENTS (L1,L2,L1/2)		
Locational action components: Other SC action		
Static (L2):		
Ever other action in beat – presence	0.007048	0.1279
Ever other action in beat – marg effect of final amount	-0.003657	0.001937
Dynamic (L1/L2):		
Ever other action in beat – presence x year trend	0.003143	0.00294
Ever other action in beat – marg effect of final amount x yr trend	0.00004314	0.00004535
Ever other action in beat – presence x global comparison trend	-0.1058	0.2813
Ever other action in beat – marg effect of final amount x global comp trend	0.006974	0.004102
Ever other action in beat – presence x Cen fam comparison trend	0.08671	0.07412
Ever other action in beat – marg effect of final amount x Census family comparison trend	0.0001142	0.001296
Safer Cities effects: Other SC action (L1)		
Other action – effect of presence on a particular beat-year	-0.007328	0.004608
Other action – marg intensity effect of amount on a particular beat-year	-0.0003664	0.0001917

Continued

Table A3.2 Fixed components in recorded crime model cont.

VARIABLE IN MODEL	COEFFICIENT ESTIMATE	STANDARD ERROR

Locational action components: Ever burglary action in beat

(special account taken, below, of any bias due to differential location
of action in **superbeats,** or beats with **incomplete series** of beat-years)

Static (L2):

– presence	0.03804	0.1101
… and in superbeat	-0.1979	0.1931
… and in beat with incomplete series	-0.3675	0.5724
– marginal-intensity effect of final amount	-0.01089	0.009531
… and in superbeat	0.03837	0.04162
… and in beat with incomplete series	-0.01852	0.02747

Dynamic (L1/L2):

– presence x year trend	-0.006362	0.002432
… and in beat with incomplete series	0.004263	0.02105
… and in superbeat	0.004797	0.00416
– marginal-intensity effect of final amount x *year* trend	-0.0002081	0.0001852
… and in beat with incomplete series	-0.0004795	0.001051
… and in superbeat	0.0009528	0.000894
– presence x **global comparison** trend	-0.3058	0.2397
… and in beat with incomplete series	0.5017	1.31
… and in superbeat	0.8289	0.4427
– marginal-intensity effect of final amount x **global comparison** trend	0.03275	0.01982
… and in beat with incomplete series	0.04266	0.06361
… and in superbeat	-0.282	0.1838
– presence x **Census family comparison** trend	0.2377	0.08011
… and in beat with incomplete series	0.2768	0.1713
… and in superbeat	-0.3426	0.1641
– marginal-intensity effect of final amount x **Census family** comparison	-0.005936	0.005385
… and in beat with incomplete series	-0.003314	0.008396
… and in superbeat	0.1405	0.09402

Safer Cities effects: SC burglary action
Burglary action – step – general effect of presence of action on a particular beat-year (L1)

	-0.01298	0.006892
… special effect in beat with no beat-years measured before action (L1/L2)	-0.01056	0.01913

Burglary action – general marginal-intensity effect of amount of action on a particular beat-year, given presence of action (L1)

	-0.001428	0.001026
… special effect in beat with no beat-years measured before action (L1/L2)	0.0006586	0.001267

NB Some of the beat-years with action were in beats with an incomplete series of measurements (i.e. <6 beat-years). Incompleteness in general was taken account of in the model, including in the locational action components. However, some of the incomplete action beats specifically had no beat-years measured **before** action was implemented. It was thus impossible to distinguish their locational effects from their Safer Cities after effects in these beats. This enabled inclusion of all available beat-years with action in the model, whilst discounting any bias due to an inability to filter out their locational effects. Of the total 734 beat-years with action in the model, 124 were from beats which had no before-measurements. As can be seen, the after effect of the **presence** of action would have been much greater if the subsidiary term had not been included (because the subsidiary shows a further substantial reduction in burglary risk). The special incompleteness effect for the **marginal** effect of action served, by contrast, to mask some of the general effect, but was modest in size and very unreliable. Excluding it from the model would have meant the general effect would have been somewhat smaller. Only the coefficients of the general terms were used in calculation of the reduction in risk, and the cost of preventing burglary.

Explanatory variables: Random components

City was originally included as Level 3, but when all variables were included in the model, the between-cities variation in the baseline constant had dropped to zero. The model was therefore simplified to two levels (beat-year and beat only). This made very little difference to the fixed coefficients or their significance.

The *Level 2* random component of the constant is the residual variation (unexplained by the fixed effects), between beats, of the burglary incidence risk. The residual for each beat is the average unexplained risk common to all beat-years for that beat. By definition, it does not change over the six–year period of measurement.

The *Level 1* random component of the constant is the residual unexplained variance of risk between beat-years.

The random components and their estimated variances are shown in Table A3.3.

Table A3.3 Random components in recorded crime model

VARIABLE IN MODEL	COEFFICIENT ESTIMATE	STANDARD ERROR
LEVEL 2 (Beats, n=701)		
Constant, between-beat variance	0.004857	0.000304
LEVEL 1 (Beat-years, n=3,277)		
Constant, for all beat-years, residual between-beat-year variance	0.003377	0.00009405

Significance testing

Significance testing for the modelling is described in Appendix 1.

The *fit* statistic measures how closely the model predicts the observed values of burglary risk over all interviews. It is calculated as -2[log(likelihood ratio)]. Larger (strictly, more positive) numbers indicate a *poorer* fit–in other words, less of the observed variation in risk is predicted or explained by the model. From a presentational perspective, it is easier to work backwards from the full model and show the decrement in fit obtained when particular terms are removed from the model. The *decrement in fit* is distributed as Chi-squared (with degrees of freedom = number of terms dropped).

The full model as a whole is tested against a 'null model', a highly cut-down version which in this case comprises:

Fixed terms: Intercept
Random terms: Level 1 (residual between-beat-years) variation of Constant
Level 2 (between-beats) variation of Constant.

The difference in the likelihood comparing the full model to the base/null model showed a decrement of *917.97, 73* df (p *<<0.00001*), derived from *-7036.66, 3* df (null) minus *-7954.63*, 76 df (full).

The results of removing particular terms from the model, are shown in Figure A3.2

Figure A3.2 Statistical significance of Safer Cities after-effects – recorded crime

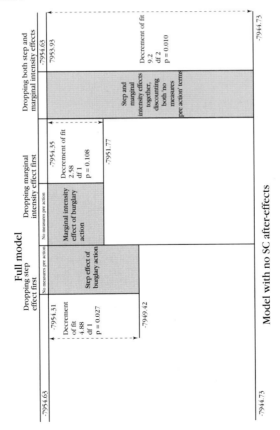

Generating expected values for display: Sample enumeration

The presentation of results in Figures 3.3 and 3.4 is based on a technique called 'sample enumeration' (Davies, 1992a,b). (This is nothing to do with survey sampling.) The aim is to generate the 'counterfactual' – values of burglary risk in the beat-years following action, which we would have *expected* to find had there been no action, but everything else remained the same. 'Everything else' means common background trends and between-area differences. Generating expected values involves several steps (equivalent to those for the survey, in Appendix 1):

i)   generating predicted (i.e. expected) burglary risk values (in [Arcsine (burglary recorded incidence risk per household)$^{-4}$] transformation) for every action beat-year, based on all explanatory variables in the entire fixed statistical model as in Table A3.2

ia) adding to this, the 'beat-level residuals' generated by ML3E – i.e. the unexplained variation in (transformed) risk between beats averaged over the whole six-year period of measurements. These residuals were incorporated to make *change over time* stand out more clearly. They collectively appear as the 'between-beat variance' of the random components in the model shown in Table A3.3

ii) generating for every action beat-year, the 'transformed adjustment factor' from the values of the terms representing the effects of Safer Cities action (both step and marginal intensity effects) in the model

iii) subtracting the latter from the former to leave the expected transformed burglary risk for each action beat-year (expected on the basis of all terms other than those representing the Safer Cities after-effect)

iv) transforming this back to incidence probability risk values

v)   [no equivalent step to ED-averaging in survey, because values already relate to area level]

vi) subtracting the expected action beat-year risk from the observed action beat-year risk, to produce the 'observed - expected' incidence probability risk for each action beat-year (O-E thus amounts to our estimate of the Safer Cities effect plus the residual, unexplained variation between *beat-years* - the unexplained residual variation between beats was incorporated in the expected values at step ia))

vii) calculating relative percent difference (RPD) as   100   [observed   -
expected] / expected

viii) then averaging observed action beat-year burglary risks over each of the
'action sets' of beats–those ending up with low, middle and high action;
doing likewise for expected risks and RPD.

It is these latter grouped averages that are presented in the figures.

The relationship between RPD and (low, medium and high) action intensity
levels in Figure 3.4 illustrates the Safer Cities effect estimated in our model,
under the particular conditions measured for each action beat in each year.
As stated in step vi), it also incorporates some of the time-based variation
unexplained in the model.

Figure A3.3 shows the same relationship of RPC with action intensity, but
this time plotted on an individual action beat-year basis for the 734 such
units. Also on the Figure is a simple linear OLS regression line showing both
the step down and the downward slope of the marginal intensity effect
identified in the model (from inspection of the scatter, rather more reliable
than its survey equivalent in Figure A1.2). It would again be interesting to
compare the anti-burglary action in beat-years falling significantly below this
line (i.e., performing better than average) with those above it (i.e.,
performing worse than average).

Figure A3.3 Recorded crime: relative percent difference in burglary incidence for each action beat-year, against action intensity

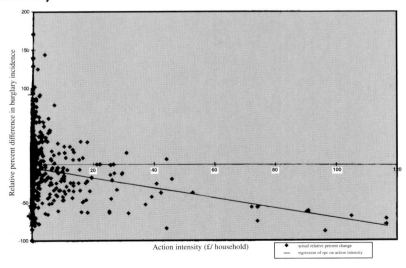

Note: One point with zero action and an extreme RPD was omitted for scaling purposes.

Calculating the estimated reductions in risk due to burglary action

The calculations to estimate the step, overall and marginal reductions in risk for the recorded crime model were performed in a similar way to those for the survey (Appendix 1). The main differences (apart, of course, from the values of the coefficients) were:

i) instead of transforming the sample incidence probability logistically (steps 2 and 3 in Appendix 1), it was transformed by the arcsine of its 4th root, then adjusted by the model coefficients, and transformed back to 'real' probabilities

ii) the effect of the prior burglary probability on the after-effects of Safer Cities burglary action was not estimated in the model, for reasons explained above.

These calculations produced Table A3.4.

Table A3.4 Recorded crime results – Reductions in burglary incidence risk associated with Safer Cities action

Baseline burglary incidence per 100 households	Step per cent reduction in risk due to **presence** of action	Marginal per cent reduction in risk **per extra £** of action	Overall per cent reduction in risk
3	11	1.1	15
5	9	1.0	13
10	7	0.8	10
15	6	0.7	9
20	6	0.6	8
25	5	0.6	7
30	5	0.5	6
35	4	0.5	6

Note: The reductions are estimated relative to the expected incidence probability on a given beat-year, in the absence of Safer Cities action. The baseline *incidence* rates in these example calculations have been chosen as equivalent to the corresponding *prevalence* rates for the survey results in Table A1.4. (For every victim in the current survey there are an average 1.5 incidents; for every surveyed incident there are an average 0.66 recorded incidents, from the 1992 British Crime Survey.) The 3% burglary incidence probability is equivalent to the national average prevalence from the British Crime Survey; the 10% incidence probability is equivalent to the average prevalence probability from the present survey.

The *step* effect is the reduction in incidence probability associated simply with the presence of Safer Cities action in the relevant beat in the relevant year. The *marginal-intensity* effect is the reduction in incidence probability per extra £1 of action per household (beyond £3.57), spent in an area at the time of original implementation. The overall effect is the reduction in incidence probability associated with the presence of Safer Cities burglary action in the area, at the average of £3.57 per household over the year, taking presence and intensity into account. The action input comprises both Safer Cities and levered funds. SC burglary action is almost always accompanied by SC other action in the beat, so these figures are more directly equivalent to the figures in brackets in Table A1.4.

Table A3.4 shows that all these proportional reductions in risk (step, marginal and overall) diminish as the baseline risk increases. In other words, it *appears* to become harder to reduce burglary in areas suffering from greater risk of the crime. However, we should be cautious about drawing this conclusion, because, unlike with the survey, we could not represent prior burglary risk directly in the statistical model for reasons already given. The effect with recorded crime observed here is likely to be a property of the mathematical transformation required to make the crime data suitable for statistical modelling; it strongly compresses differences in the baseline at low levels of risk.

At a 10 per cent incidence level of risk (equivalent to the average prevalence risk in the survey) *the mere presence of Safer Cities burglary action seemed to reduce the risk of burglary by about seven per cent.* On the marginal impact, *given the presence of action at the average intensity (£3.57), for an additional £1 of action the risk of burglary fell by a further 0.8 per cent.* Step and marginal-intensity effects combined showed an *overall reduction of some ten per cent* at the average action intensity.

Cost–effectiveness calculations for the recorded crime findings

These again followed the same procedure as for the survey (Appendix 1), and used the same cost figures for overheads and duration of impact. Because we were dealing directly with incidence there was no need to convert from prevalence. However, costs were *divided by 1.5* to convert them from cost per recorded incident prevented, to cost per 'real' incident prevented, taking account of the shortfall of recording of burglaries. We costed the step effect at the average action input of £3.57. Since we again had to take account of other Safer Cities action, which was present in virtually every beat with Safer Cities burglary action, we costed this at the average input of £7.73. In total, the average input associated with the presence of Safer Cities burglary action, plus other supporting action, was £11.30 per household. This included levered funds.

Estimating the total gross gain from Safer Cities domestic burglary prevention

Some £4.4million of Safer Cities funds were spent directly on domestic burglary prevention through the 500 schemes implemented over the Programme's lifetime. But some 10 per cent of this was spent on 'citywide' anti-burglary schemes, such as publicity–so removing these gives an adjusted figure of £4million. If all the local anti-burglary schemes enjoyed extra levered funds in the same proportion as the 300 for which we had data in the evaluation (an average £67 of leverage per £100 Safer Cities funds), then the total money spent from all sources on the local schemes would have been (£4m x 1.67 =) £6.6 million.

We now divide this total by the overall cost of reducing one burglary, to get a rough estimate of the total number of burglaries directly prevented by Safer Cities action. We use the recorded crime cost based on Safer Cities and levered funds, and take the particular cost estimate calculated from our model, for a 'real' incidence of 10 incidents/100 households, i.e. £552. (This incidence is a reasonable figure for 'city' conditions typical of those in which Safer Cities burglary action was implemented.) But this figure has to be adjusted by removal of two factors taken into account in estimating the £552 cost per burglary prevented: the £552 takes account of both the domestic burglary cost element (average intensity £3.57 per household) and the 'other Safer Cities action' element (£7.73 per household). We wish to remove the latter. The adjustment for this is to multiply by the ratio of average burglary action intensity to average total action intensity:

x 3.57 / (3.57 + 7.73)

The £552 also includes Safer Cities overheads at 50p per pound spent on scheme funding. The adjustment to remove this is x 1 / 1.5.

The total adjusted cost per burglary prevented, in direct local anti-burglary scheme funds, is £552 x 0.21 = £116.26. This includes levered money.

Dividing this figure into £6.6 million gives over 56,000 burglaries prevented.

If each burglary prevented had a total (direct and indirect) cost of prevention of £552, and avoided a cost to victims and the state of £1,100, then it represented a saving of £548.

Multiplying this saving by 56,000 burglaries prevented gives a rough estimate of £31million saved by the £4 million (plus £2.6m leverage) spent on local Safer Cities domestic burglary schemes.

Appendix 4: Differences between the statistical models of survey and recorded crime data

Table A4.1 lists the differences between the survey and recorded crime analyses.

Survey analysis	Recorded crime analysis
Data units	
interview/individual households /EDs (200hh)	beat-year/beat (1700hh)/(city)
Time	
before-after	6 year time series (up to 6 beat-years per beat)
Outcome (dependent) variable	
yes/no victimisation per interview surveyed	incidence rate per beat-year recorded
excluded attempt burglaries	partial inclusion of attempts
Sampling	
embedded panel of households/ selected high crime EDs/SC and matched cities (10 + 8)	most beat years/almost all beats/ SC and cities (14 + 9)
Comparison	
surveys in SC EDs with no action, and in matched comparison cities alike	no-action beat-years/almost all beats SC and matched cities (14 +9)
Statistical model	
logistic (victim/non victim prevalence) 3 level	arcsin (incidence risk rate)$^{1/4}$ 2-level
Variables in model	
prior ED burglary prevalence risk as explanatory variable	not in model
action presence and intensity/interactions with prior burglary prevalence risk	action presence and intensity
simple locational (main) effects of action	complex locational effects of action: static/3 dynamic indicators
wide range of individual and ED demographic variables	relatively narrow range of beat and city demographic variables

Several of the differences in Table A4.1 (or their consequences in terms of the Safer Cities action that was actually sampled in the two analyses) were felt to be worth discussing to facilitate interpretation of the findings.

Size of area. It is well-known in geography that relationships found between measured features of territories of a particular size (such as the link between crime levels in a set of territories and the number of young people residing there) will be different when territories that are smaller, or larger, are studied. This is known as the 'modifiable areal unit problem' (Openshaw, 1984). Some of the relationships will grow or shrink, or reverse direction; some existing ones will disappear and new ones appear. So in this respect, finding different results between survey and recorded crime analyses is not surprising, given the beats had on average ten times the population of the surveyed EDs. One specific way in which size of territory studied could have affected the results is through measurement of displacement or diffusion of benefit.

The larger territories of beats meant that the estimates we did produce are likely to be net of any displacement which merely moved burglaries around within the beats. (In many cases, action covered only part of a beat, which was less likely with the surveyed EDs.) By the same token, diffusion of benefit would be more likely to be felt within the beat rather than outside it. In both cases, cost estimates are partially net of displacement or diffusion. Surveyed EDs, being smaller, would have been far more likely to export their unintended effects. Estimates from the survey would be more likely to be gross, i.e. excluding any displacement or diffusion. 'Internal displacement' within beats would have meant our cost estimates from recorded crime were *overstated* relative to those from the survey. This is because the net reduction in burglary, combining the main and displacement effects of action, would be smaller for a given input of action, than the gross reduction. Any burglaries displaced into comparison areas would (as discussed in Chapter 2) further overstate the cost estimate. 'Internal diffusion of benefit' would have meant the recorded crime cost estimates were *understated* relative to the survey. On these grounds, the larger size of the beat tends to give us something approaching a better *net* estimate of the cost of preventing a burglary; the survey a better gross *estimate*.

The average action intensity in beats (£3.57 for action beat-years) was markedly lower than that for the surveyed EDs (£16.00 for EDs with action). This was because the larger territories of beats meant that action more often only covered part of a beat, dilution rendering the average figure per household smaller.

Whatever the case, this difference in average action intensity may square with the fact that the average overall reduction in *risk* associated with action was also lower in the beats (some 10% at the 'real' incidence risk of 10 per hundred households) than in the surveyed EDs (29%). The overall cost estimates for survey and recorded crime nevertheless came out similar because the latter's lower reduction in risk was associated with a lower average intensity of action.

Size of schemes in the sampled areas. In the survey analysis, there was a significant bias in our sample towards larger schemes, which either covered more households and/or spent more (although their action was no more intense). This may have given strength to the step effect (of the mere presence of action) at the expense of the marginal-intensity effect.

Sampling households in areas versus sampling areas alone. The survey measured outcome by sampling individual households in each ED, and then deriving area prevalence risks from the sample. The recorded crime approach directly measured area incidence risks. 'Sampling error' would make the measured survey risks less reliable at the ED level, due to the small numbers of households surveyed in each. The survey would also be vulnerable to the vagaries of hitting or missing individual households which had received action. It is possible that this measurement issue hindered the detection of any marginal-intensity effect of action in the statistical model, meaning the recorded crime model was more sensitive.

Reporting of burglaries to the police. A possibility sometimes considered in evaluating crime prevention is that a scheme's impact on the risk of crime may be masked by its effect in encouraging victims more often to report the crimes they have suffered to the police. Surveys are of course unaffected by any such process. There was limited evidence from the survey that, if anything, the opposite was the case. We asked burglary victims in the survey whether they had reported the incident to the police (or the latest incident, if several). There was no change from before to after in the rate of reporting in the comparison cities. Overall, there was an increase of some four per cent in the Safer Cities. Respondents in the Safer Cities EDs receiving low and medium action did show an increase in reporting (12% and 7% respectively) but those in the high action band showed a marked decrease in reporting of 19 per cent. Any such decrease would mimic or amplify a Safer Cities effect, meaning the recorded crime marginal cost estimate could be too low. However, the evidence is not strong, due to the relatively small numbers of victims (115, 62 and 81 respectively in the three action sets), the inconsistent nature of the pattern, and the selected nature of the survey areas. But it is somewhat puzzling. We did attempt to circumvent the 'small numbers of victims' problem by asking all respondents whether they would have reported a burglary had they suffered one, but the 'yes' responses were so predominant that it proved impossible to look for any change in response differentially associated with Safer Cities action. Altogether, we can conclude that there is very limited evidence that the recorded crime estimate may have been inflated by a decrease in reporting to the police in high action beats, cause unknown.

References

Barr, R. and **Pease, K.** (1990). 'Crime placement, displacement and deflection.' **In Tonry, M.** and **Morris, N.** (Eds.) *Crime and Justice: A Review of Research,* vol. 12. Chicago: University of Chicago Press.

Barr, R. and **Pease, K.** (1992). 'A place for every crime and every crime in its place.' In **Evans, D. J., Fyfe, N. R.** and **Herbert, D. T.** (Eds.) *Crime, Policing and Place: Essays in Environmental Criminology.* London: Routledge.

Brantingham, P.J. and **Brantingham, P.L.** (1991). *Environmental Criminology.* Prospect Heights, Illinois: Waveland Press.

Bryk, A. and **Raudenbush, S.** (1992). *Hierarchical Linear Models. Applications and Data Analysis Methods.* Newbury Park: Sage.

Campbell, D. T. and **Stanley, J. C.** (1963). *Experimental and Quasi-Experimental Designs in Social Research.* Chicago: Rand McNally.

Carnie, J. (1995). *The Safer Cities Programme in Scotland:* Overview Report. London: HMSO.

Clarke, R. V. and **Weisburd, D.** (1994). 'Diffusion of crime control benefits: Observations on the reverse of displacement' in *Crime Prevention Studies 2.* Monsey, NY: Criminal Justice Press.

Cook, T. D. and **Campbell, D. T.** (1979). *Quasi-Experimentation.* Chicago: Rand McNally.

Craig, J. (1985). *A 1981 Socio-economic Classification of Local and Health Authorities of Great Britain.* OPCS Studies of Medical and Population Subjects 48. London: HMSO.

Davidson, N. (1984). *'Burglary in the community: patterns of localisation in offender-victim relations',* in **Clarke, R.** and **Hope, T.** (Eds.), Coping with Burglary: Research Perspectives on Policy pp 61-75. Boston: Kleuer Nijhoff.

Davies, R. (1992a). *'The state of the art in survey analysis.'* In **Westlake, A., Banks, R., Payne, C.** and **Orchard, T.** (Eds). Survey and Statistical Computing. New York: North-Holland.

Davies, R..(1992b). *'Sample enumeration methods for model interpretation.'* In van der **Heijden, P., Jansen,W. Francis, B.** and **Seeber, G.** (Eds.) Statistical Modelling. Amsterdam: Elsevier.

Department of the Environment (1995). **1991 Deprivation Index**: *a Review of Approaches and a Matrix of Results.* London: HMSO.

Ekblom, P. (1990). *'Evaluating crime prevention: the management of uncertainty.'* In **Kemp, C.** (Ed.) Current Issues in Criminological Research. Bristol: Bristol Centre for Criminal Justice.

Ekblom, P. (1991). *High Crime Areas, Crime Surveys and Evaluation:* the *Safer Cities Programme.* Paper presented at the Third British Criminology Conference, York, July. (Available from author.)

Ekblom, P. (1992). *'The Safer Cities Programme impact evaluation: problems and progress.'* Studies on Crime and Crime Prevention 1: 35-51.

Ekblom, P. (1994). *'Scoping and scoring: Linking measures of action to measures of outcome in a multi-scheme, multi-site crime prevention programme'*. In **Zahm, D.** and **Cromwell, P.** (Eds.) *Proceedings of the International Seminar on Environmental Criminology and Crime Analysis,* University of Miami, May 1993. Florida Statistical Analysis Center / Florida Criminal Justice Executive institute.

Ekblom, P., Howes, D. and **Law, H.** 1994. *Scoping, Scoring and Modelling:* Linking Measures of Crime Preventive Action to Measures of Outcome in a Large, Multi-site Evaluation using a GIS and Multilevel Modelling. Paper presented at GIS Research UK 1994, Leicester University, 12 April. (Available from first author.)

Ekblom, P., Law, H. and **Arthur, S.** (in preparation). *The Safer Cities Programme:* Nature and Range of its Action.

Ekblom, P. and **Pease, K.** (1995). *'Evaluating crime prevention.'* In **Tonry, M.** and **Farrington, D.** (Eds.), *Building a Safer Society:* Strategic Approaches to Crime Prevention. *Crime and Justice:* A Review of Research, vol. 19. London and Chicago, University of Chicago Press, pp. 585-662.

Ekblom, P., Sutton, M. And **Law, H.** (1996). *Safer Cities and Domestic Burglary.* Research Finding 42. London: Home Office.

Ekblom, P., Sutton, M. and **Wiggins, R.** (1993). *Scoping, Scoring and Modelling:* Linking Measures of Crime Preventive Action to Measures of Outcome in a Large, Multi-Site Evaluation. Talk to Royal Statistical Society, London, December 1993 (available from author).

Farrell, G. and **Pease, K.** (1994). *Once Bitten, Twice Bitten:* Repeat Victimisation and its Implications for Crime Prevention. Home Office Crime Prevention Unit Paper 46. London: Home Office.

Farrell, G. (1995). *Preventing repeat victimisation.* In **Tonry, M.** and **Farrington, D.** (Eds.), *Building a Safer Society:* Strategic Approaches to Crime Prevention. *Crime and Justice: A Review of Research, vol. 19.* London and Chicago, University of Chicago Press, pp. 469-534.

Forrester, D., Chatterton, M. and **Pease, K.** (1988). *The Kirkholt Burglary Prevention Demonstration Project.* Crime Prevention Unit Paper 13. London: Home Office.

Forrester, D., Frenz, S., O'Connell, M. and **Pease, K.** (1990). *The Kirkholt Burglary Prevention Project: Phase II.* Crime Prevention Unit Paper 23. London: Home Office.

Foster, J. and **Hope, T.** (1993). *Housing, Community and Crime: the Impact of the Priority Estates Project.* Home Office Research Study 131. London: HMSO.

Goldstein, Harvey (1995). *Multilevel Statistical Models.* London: Edward Arnold; NY: Halsted Press.

Hesseling, R. (1994). *'Displacement: a review of the empirical literature'* In **Clarke, R. V.** (Ed.), *Crime Prevention Studies 3.* Monsey, NY: Criminal Justice Press.

Home Office (1990a). *Crime Prevention: the Success of the Partnership Approach.* Home Office Circular 44/90. London: Home Office.

Home Office (1990b). *Safer Cities Progress Report,* 1989–1990. London: Home Office.

Home Office (1991). *Safer Cities Progress Report,* 1990–1991. London: Home Office.

Home Office (1993a). *A Practical Guide to Crime Prevention for Local Partnerships,* prepared by Crime Concern. London: Home Office.

Home Office (1993b). *Safer Cities Progress Report, 1991–1992.* London: Home Office.

Howes, D. (1994). *Scoping and Scoring Analysis System: User Guide.* Lancaster: North West Regional Research Laboratory, University of Lancaster. (Available from Paul Ekblom)

Jones, K. (1992). *'Multi-level Modeling'.* In **Westlake, A., Banks, R., Payne, C.** and **Orchard, T.** (Eds). *Survey and Statistical Computing.* New York: North-Holland.

Judd, C. M. and **Kenny, D. A.** (1981). *Estimating the Effects of Social Interventions.* New York: Cambridge University Press.

Junger-Tas, J. (1993). *'Policy evaluation research in criminal justice'. Studies on Crime and Crime Prevention vol 2,* pp 7-20. Stockholm, Sweden: National Council for Crime Prevention.

Laycock, G.K. (1985). *Property Marking: a deterrent to domestic burglary? Crime Prevention Unit Paper 3.* London: Home Office.

Laycock, G. K. (1992). *'Operation Identification or the power of publicity?'* in **RV Clarke** (Ed.), *Crime Prevention: Successful Case Studies.* New York: Harrow and Heston.

Laycock, G. and **Tilley, N.** (1995). *'Implementing crime prevention.'* In **Tonry, M.** and **Farrington, D.** (Eds.), Building a Safer Society: *Strategic Approaches to Crime Prevention. Crime and Justice: A Review of Research, vol. 19.* London and Chicago, University of Chicago Press pp 535-584.

Liddle, M. and **Bottoms, A.E.** (1992). *Implementing Circular 8/84: A Retrospective Assessment of the 5 Towns Initiative.* Unpublished report to Home Office, available from Institute of Criminology, Cambridge.

Maguire, M. (1982). *Burglary in a Dwelling.* London: Heinemann.

Mark, M. (1983). *'Treatment implementation, statistical power and internal validity.'* Evaluation Review, vol 7, pp 543-549.

MORI (1990). *Safer Cities Survey 1990 Technical Report.* London: Market and Opinion Research International.

MORI (1993). *Safer Cities Survey 1992 Technical Report.* London: Market and Opinion Research International.

Openshaw, S. (1984). *The Modifiable Areal Unit Problem.* Norwich: Geobooks.

Osborn, S. and **Shaftoe, H.** (1995). *Safer Neighbourhoods? Successes and Failures in Crime Prevention.* London: SNU (summarised as Housing *Research Findings 149.* York: Joseph Rowntree Foundation.)

Pawson, R. and **Tilley, N.** (1994). *'What works in evaluation research?'*. *British Journal of Criminology.* 34, 1994, pp 291-306.

Polder, W. (1992). *Crime Prevention in The Netherlands:* Pilot Projects Evaluated. *Dutch Penal Law and Policy* 7. The Hague, Netherlands: Research and Documentation Centre.

Prosser, R., Rasbash, J. and **Goldstein, H.** (1991). ML3: *Software for Three-Level Analysis, Users' Guide for V.2.* London: Institute of Education, University of London.

Rhodes, W. and **C. Conly** (1981). *'Crime and mobility: an empirical study.'* In: **P. Brantingham** and **P. Brantingham** (Eds.), Environmental Criminology. Beverly Hills: Sage.

SCPR. (1993). *1992 British Crime Survey Technical Report.* London, Social and community planning research.

Skogan, W. (1990). *Disorder and Decline: Crime and the Spiral of Decay in American Neighborhoods.* New York: Free Press.

Sutton, M. (1996, in press). *Implementing crime prevention schemes in a multi-agency setting: aspects of process in the Safer Cities Programme.* Home Office Research Study (in preparation). London, HMSO.

Tilley, N. (1992). *Safer Cities and Community Safety Strategies. Crime Prevention Unit Paper 38.* London: Home Office.

Tilley, N. (1993a). *Understanding Car Parks, Crime and CCTV: Evaluation Lessons from Safer Cities.* Home Office Crime Prevention Unit Paper 42. London: Home Office.

Tilley, N. (1993b). *'Crime prevention and the Safer Cities story',* Howard Journal of Criminal Justice, vol 32 pp 32-57.

Tilley, N. and **Webb, J.** (1994). Burglary Reduction: *Findings from Safer Cities Schemes.* Home Office Crime Prevention Unit Paper 51. London: Home Office.

Trickett, A., Osborn, D., Seymour, J. And **Pease, K.** (1992). *'What is different about high-crime areas?'*. British Journal of Criminology, vol 32/1, pp 81-89.

Wright, R., R. Logie, and **S. Decker** (1995). *'Criminal expertise and offender decision making:* an experimental study of the target selection process in residential burglary'. *Journal of Research in Crime and Delinquency,* vol 32, pp 39-53.

Youell, J. (1993). *Assessment and Monitoring of Safer Cities Schemes: A Guidance Manual for Project Staff.* London: Police Research Group, Home Office.

Publications

List of research publications

A list of research reports for the last three years is provided below. A **full** list of publications is available on request from the Research and Statistics Directorate Information and Publications Group

Home Office Research Studies (HORS)

133. **Intensive Probation in England and Wales: an evaluation.** George Mair, Charles Lloyd, Claire Nee and Rae Sibbett. 1994. xiv + 143pp. (0 11 341114 6).

134. **Contacts between Police and Public: findings from the 1992 British Crime Survey.** Wesley G Skogan. 1995. ix + 93pp. (0 11 341115 4).

135. **Policing low-level disorder: Police use of Section 5 of the Public Order Act 1986.** David Brown and Tom Ellis. 1994. ix + 69pp. (0 11 341116 2).

136. **Explaining reconviction rates: A critical analysis.** Charles Lloyd, George Mair and Mike Hough. 1995. xiv + 103pp. (0 11 341117 0).

137. **Case Screening by the Crown Prosecution Service: How and why cases are terminated.** Debbie Crisp and David Moxon. 1995. viii + 66pp. (0 11 341137 5).

138. **Public Interest Case Assessment Schemes.** Debbie Crisp, Claire Whittaker and Jessica Harris. 1995. x + 58pp. (0 11 341139 1).

139. **Policing domestic violence in the 1990s.** Sharon Grace. 1995. x + 74pp. (0 11 341140 5).

140. **Young people, victimisation and the police: British Crime Survey findings on experiences and attitudes of 12 to 15 year olds.** Natalie Aye Maung. 1995. xii + 140pp. (0 11 341150 2).

141. **The Settlement of refugees in Britain.** Jenny Carey-Wood, Karen Duke, Valerie Karn and Tony Marshall. 1995. xii + 133pp. (0 11 341145 6).

142. **Vietnamese Refugees since 1982.** Karen Duke and Tony Marshall. 1995. x + 62pp. (0 11 341147 2).

143. **The Parish Special Constables Scheme.** Peter Southgate, Tom Bucke and Carole Byron. 1995. x + 59pp. (1 85893 458 3).

144. **Measuring the Satisfaction of the Courts with the Probation Service.** Chris May. 1995. x + 76pp. (1 85893 483 4).

145. **Young people and crime.** John Graham and Benjamin Bowling. 1995. xv + 142pp. (1 85893 551 2).

146. **Crime against retail and manufacturing premises: findings from the 1994 Commercial Victimisation Survey.** Catriona Mirrlees-Black and Alec Ross. 1995. xi + 110pp. (1 85893 554 7).

147. **Anxiety about crime: findings from the 1994 British Crime Survey.** Michael Hough. 1995. viii + 92pp. (1 85893 553 9).

148. **The ILPS Methadone Prescribing Project.** Rae Sibbitt. 1996. viii + 69pp. (1 85893 485 0).

149. **To scare straight or educate? The British experience of day visits to prison for young people.** Charles Lloyd. 1996. xi + 60pp. (1 85893 570 9).

150. **Predicting reoffending for Discretionary Conditional Release.** John B Copas, Peter Marshall and Roger Tarling. 1996. vii + 49pp. (1 85893 576 8).

151. **Drug misuse declared: results of the 1994 British Crime Survey.** Malcom Ramsay and Andrew Percy. 1996. xv + 131pp. (1 85893 628 4).

152. **An Evaluation of the Introduction and Operation of the Youth Court.** David O'Mahony and Kevin Haines. 1996. viii + 70pp. (1 85893 579 2).

153. **Fitting supervision to offenders: assessment and allocation decisions in the Probation Service.** Ros Burnett. 1996. xi + 99pp. (1 85893 599 7).

154. **Ethnic minorities: victimisation and racial harassment. Findings from the 1988 and 1992 British Crime Surveys**. Marian Fitzgerald and Chris Hale. 1996. xi + 97pp. (1 85893 603 9).

155. **PACE ten years on: a review of the literature.** David Brown. 1997. xx + 280pp. (1 85893 603 9).

156. **Automatic Conditional Release: the first two years.** Mike Maguire, Brigitte Perroud and Peter Raynor. 1996. x + 114pp. (1 85893 659 4).

157. **Testing obscenity: an international comparison of laws and controls relating to obscene material.** Sharon Grace. 1996. ix + 46pp. (1 85893 672 1).

158. **Enforcing community sentences: supervisors' perspectives on ensuring compliance and dealing with breach.** Tom Ellis, Carol Hedderman and Ed Mortimer. 1996. x + 81pp. (1 85893 691 8).

160. **Implementing crime prevention schemes in a multi-agency setting: aspects of process in the Safer Cities programme.** Mike Sutton. 1996. x + 53pp. (1 85893 691 8).

161. **Reducing criminality among young people: a sample of relevant programmes in the United Kingdom.** David Utting. 1997. vi + 122pp. (1 85893 744 2).

162. **Imprisoned women and mothers**. Diane Caddle and Debbie Crisp. 1997. xiv + 74pp. (1 85893 760 4).

163. **Curfew orders with electronic monitoring: an evaluation of the first twelve months of the trials in Greater Manchester, Norfolk and Berkshire, 1995 - 1996**. George Mair and Ed Mortimer. 1996. x + 50pp. (1 85893 765 5).

164. **Safer cities and domestic burglaries**. Paul Ekblom, Ho Law, Mike Sutton, with assistance from Paul Crisp and Richard Wiggins. 1996. xxii + 158pp. (1 85893 894 5). **Not on general circulation.**

165. **Enforcing financial penalties.** Claire Whittaker and Alan Mackie. 1997. xii + 58pp. (1 85893 786 8).

166. **Assessing offenders' needs: assessment scales for the probation service.** Rosumund Aubrey and Michael Hough. x + 55pp.(1 85893 799 X).

168. **Managing courts effectively: The reasons for adjournments in magistrates' courts**. Claire Whittaker, Alan Mackie, Ruth Lewis and Nicola Ponikiewski. 1997. x + 37pp. (1 85893 804 X).

Nos 159 and 167 not published yet.

Research and Planning Unit Papers (RPUP)

81. **The welfare needs of unconvicted prisoners.** Diane Caddle and Sheila White. 1994.

82. **Racially motivated crime: a British Crime Survey analysis.** Natalie Aye Maung and Catriona Mirrlees-Black. 1994.

83. **Mathematical models for forecasting Passport demand.** Andy Jones and John MacLeod. 1994.

84. **The theft of firearms**. John Corkery. 1994.

85. **Equal opportunities and the Fire Service.** Tom Bucke. 1994.

86. **Drug Education Amongst Teenagers: a 1992 British Crime Survey Analysis**. Lizanne Dowds and Judith Redfern. 1995.

87. **Group 4 Prisoner Escort Service: a survey of customer satisfaction.** Claire Nee. 1994.

88. **Special Considerations: Issues for the Management and Organisation of the Volunteer Police.** Catriona Mirrlees-Black and Carole Byron. 1995.

89. **Self-reported drug misuse in England and Wales: findings from the 1992 British Crime Survey.** Joy Mott and Catriona Mirrlees-Black. 1995.

90. **Improving bail decisions: the bail process project, phase 1.** John Burrows, Paul Henderson and Patricia Morgan. 1995.

91. **Practitioners' views of the Criminal Justice Act: a survey of criminal justice agencies.** George Mair and Chris May. 1995.

92. **Obscene, threatening and other troublesome telephone calls to women in England and Wales: 1982-1992.** Wendy Buck, Michael Chatterton and Ken Pease. 1995.

93. **A survey of the prisoner escort and custody service provided by Group 4 and by Securicor Custodial Services.** Diane Caddle. 1995.

Research Findings

8. **Findings from the International Crime Survey.** Pat Mayhew. 1994.

9 **Fear of Crime: Findings from the 1992 British Crime Survey.** Catriona Mirrlees-Black and Natalie Aye Maung. 1994.

10. **Does the Criminal Justice system treat men and women differently?** Carol Hedderman and Mike Hough. 1994.

11. **Participation in Neighbourhood Watch: Findings from the 1992 British Crime Survey.** Lizanne Dowds and Pat Mayhew. 1994.

12. **Explaining Reconviction Rates: A Critical Analysis.** Charles Lloyd, George Mair and Mike Hough. 1995.

13. **Equal opportunities and the Fire Service.** Tom Bucke. 1994.

14. **Trends in Crime: Findings from the 1994 British Crime Survey.** Pat Mayhew, Catriona Mirrlees-Black and Natalie Aye Maung. 1994.

15. **Intensive Probation in England and Wales: an evaluation.** George Mair, Charles Lloyd, Claire Nee and Rae Sibbitt. 1995.

16. **The settlement of refugees in Britain.** Jenny Carey-Wood, Karen Duke, Valerie Karn and Tony Marshall. 1995.

17. **Young people, victimisation and the police: British Crime Survey findings on experiences and attitudes of 12- to 15- year-olds.** Natalie Aye Maung. 1995.

18. **Vietnamese Refugees since 1982.** Karen Duke and Tony Marshall. 1995.

19. **Supervision of Restricted Patients in the Community.** Suzanne Dell and Adrian Grounds. 1995.

20. **Videotaping children's evidence: an evaluation.** Graham Davies, Clare Wilson, Rebecca Mitchell and John Milsom. 1995.

21. **The mentally disordered and the police.** Graham Robertson, Richard Pearson and Robert Gibb. 1995.

22. **Preparing records of taped interviews.** Andrew Hooke and Jim Knox. 1995.

23. **Obscene, threatening and other troublesome telephone calls to women: Findings from the British Crime Survey.** Wendy Buck, Michael Chatterton and Ken Pease. 1995.

24. **Young people and crime.** John Graham and Ben Bowling. 1995.

25. **Anxiety about crime: Findings from the 1994 British Crime Survey.** Michael Hough. 1995.

26. **Crime against retail premises in 1993.** Catriona Mirrlees-Black and Alec Ross. 1995.

27. **Crime against manufacturing premises in 1993.** Catriona Mirrlees-Black and Alec Ross. 1995.

28. **Policing and the public: findings from the 1994 British Crime Survey.** Tom Bucke. 1995.

29. **The Child Witness Pack – An Evaluation.** Joyce Plotnikoff and Richard Woolfson. 1995.

30. **To scare straight or educate? The British experience of day visits to prison for young people.** Charles Lloyd. 1996.

31. **The ADT drug treatment programme at HMP Downview – a preliminary evaluation.** Elaine Player and Carol Martin. 1996.

32. **Wolds remand prison – an evaluation.** Keith Bottomley, Adrian James, Emma Clare and Alison Liebling. 1996.

33. **Drug misuse declared: results of the 1994 British Crime Survey.** Malcolm Ramsay and Andrew Percy. 1996.

34. **Crack cocaine and drugs-crime careers.** Howard Parker and Tim Bottomley. 1996.

35. **Imprisonment for fine default.** David Moxon and Claire Whittaker. 1996.

36. **Fine impositions and enforcement following the Criminal Justice Act 1993.** Elizabeth Charman, Bryan Gibson, Terry Honess and Rod Morgan. 1996.

37. **Victimisation in prisons.** Ian O'Donnell and Kimmett Edgar. 1996.

39. **Ethnic minorities, victimisation and racial harassment.** Marian Fitzgerald and Chris Hale. 1996.

40. **Evaluating joint performance management between the police and the Crown Prosecution Service.** Andrew Hooke, Jim Knox and David Portas. 1996.

41. **Public attitudes to drug-related crime.** Sharon Grace. 1996.

42. **Domestic burglary schemes in the Safer Cities programme.** Paul Ekblom, Ho Law and Mike Sutton. 1996.

43. **Pakistani women's experience of domestic violence in Great Britain.** Salma Choudry. 1996.

44. **Witnesses with learning disabilities.** Andrew Sanders, Jane Creaton, Sophia Bird and Leanne Weber. 1997.

45. **Does treating sex offenders reduce reoffending?** Carol Hedderman and Darren sugg. 1996.

46. **Re-education programmes for violent men - an evaluation.** Russell Dobash, Rebecca Emerson Dobash, Kate Cavanagh and Ruth Lewis. 1996.

47. **Sentencing without a pre-sentence report.** Nigel Charles, Claire Whittaker and Caroline Ball. 1997.

49. **PACE ten years on: a review of the research.** David Brown. 1997.

53. **A reconviction study of HMP Grendon Therapeutic Community.** Peter Marshall. 1997.

55. **The prevalence of convictions for sexual offending.** Peter Marshall. 1997.

Nos 50 - 52 and 54 not yet published.

Occasional Papers

Measurement of caseload weightings associated with the Children Act. Richard J. Gadsden and Graham J. Worsdale. 1994. (Available from the RSD Information and Publications Group).

Managing difficult prisoners: The Lincoln and Hull special units. Professor Keith Bottomley, Professor Norman Jepson, Mr Kenneth Elliott and Dr Jeremy Coid. 1994. (Available from the RSD Information and Publications Group).

The Nacro diversion initiative for mentally disturbed offenders: an account and an evaluation. Home Office, NACRO and Mental Health Foundation. 1994. (Available from the RSD Information and Publications Group).

Probation Motor Projects in England and Wales. J P Martin and Douglas Martin. 1994.

Community-based treatment of sex offenders: an evaluation of seven treatment programmes. R Beckett, A Beech, D Fisher and A S Fordham. 1994.

Videotaping children's evidence: an evaluation. Graham Davies, Clare Wilson, Rebecca Mitchell and John Milsom. 1995.

Managing the needs of female prisoners. Allison Morris, Chris Wilkinson, Andrea Tisi, Jane Woodrow and Ann Rockley. 1995.

Local information points for volunteers. Michael Locke, Nick Richards, Lorraine Down, Jon Griffiths and Roger Worgan. 1995.

Mental disorder in remand prisoners. Anthony Maden, Caecilia J. A. Taylor, Deborah Brooke and John Gunn. 1996.

An evaluation of prison work and training. Frances Simon and Claire Corbett. 1996.

The Impact of the National Lottery on the Horse-Race Betting Levy. Simon Field. 1996.

Requests for Publications

Home Office Research Studies from 143 onwards, *Research and Planning Unit Papers, Research Findings and Research Bulletins* are available **subject to availability** on request from:

Research and Statistics Directorate
Information and Publications Group
Room 201, Home Office
50 Queen anne's Gate
London
SW1H 9AT
Telephone: 0171-273 2084
Fascimile: 0171-222-0211
Internet: http://www.open.gov.uk/home_off/rsd/rsdhome.htm
E-mail: rsd.ho.apollo@gtnet.gov.uk

Occasional Papers can be purchased from (unless otherwise specified):
Home Office
Publications Unit
50 Queen Anne's Gate
London SW1H 9AT
Telephone: 0171 273 2302

Home Office Research Studies prior to 143 can be purchased from:

HMSO Publications Centre

(Mail, fax and telephone orders only)
PO Box 276, London SW8 5DT
Telephone orders: 0171-873 9090
General enquiries: 0171-873 0011
(queuing system in operation for both numbers)
Fax orders: 0171-873 8200

And also from **HMSO Bookshops**